BECOMING UNSTUCK

MOVING ON FROM THE DYSFUNCTION OF FAMILY HISTORY

Discover how past events control present choices.
Discover how to become unstuck and move on.

PETER BRUNTON

Published by Northwest Media
5495 Clarcona-Ocoee Rd, Orlando, Fl. 32810
www.northwestorlando.com

Printed in the United States of America

ISBN: 978-0-578-58592-5

All Scripture quotations, unless otherwise indicated, are taken from **THE HOLY BIBLE, NEW INTERNATIONAL VERSION®, NIV® Copyright © 1973, 1978, 1984, 2011 by Biblica, Inc.® Used by permission. All rights reserved worldwide.**

Scripture quotations marked (KJV) are taken from the KING JAMES VERSION, public domain.

Table of Contents

~

Acknowledgments

My deepest thanks first and foremost to my family— to my mother
and father for modeling such excellent character, to my wife for being
a challenger and a cheerleader, to my in-laws for being ecclesiastical
disrupters, and to my children for catching what has been passed to
me.

My mentors, my church, my friends, my editor, Marti, and to all
who have cheered me along this path to writing my first book. Thank
you all.

Note

Some names and identifying details have been changed to protect
the privacy of individuals. This book is not intended as a substitute
for professional counseling but rather supplemental. The reader
should consider consulting a counsellor/pastor/rabbi in matters relat-
ing to his/her emotional and spiritual health.

The Day I Found a Gap

Three o'clock in the morning, and I still wasn't asleep. I had been tossing for hours and couldn't shut off my brain. Nights like this had dogged me for over a year now, and I had good reason to chalk it up to a difficult season of life—no more, no less. My dad had died more than a year before, losing his two-year battle against cancer.

I felt cheated for him. I felt cheated for me. After he'd given so much for the church, I thought he deserved better from God. But I was no different from anyone who goes through mourning and the life that happens after it. *I mean, come on, Pete! Your dad wasn't the first to die and won't be the last. Get on with life, for Pete's sake. Quite literally: for Pete's sake.*

Yes, I had to move on, but this particular night was the start of a discovery I didn't yet understand.

I got up to go for a walk around the neighborhood and decided to talk with God. My mind was racing, stringing all my thoughts into one continuous argument. My main concern was that my wife, Crystal, and I were planning a family. I knew I had to get our finances in order so we could buy a house, especially since real estate prices were skyrocketing.

How am I gonna come up with the money for a house when I blew my savings going to Scotland to be with my sick dad? And my church salary's nothing to write home about. Even though we're growing, we aren't bringing in much while we fix up our old building. Anyway, how can I ever make real money when the last thing God told me to do was to be here and build this church?

"God, You're the worst-paying boss," I blurted out.

Wow. I had said it. I wasn't shocked; it was how I felt. I knew I was doing what God had called me to do, but He wasn't making it easy for me, and I felt like a big fat failure. Instantly, I had a response to my statement:

"It's not My fault," I heard Him say in my head.

Why does God have to be so cryptic? What does that even mean? Was it my fault? Was it someone else's fault? What do I do with an answer like that? But I knew I had to figure it out.

It took time, but as I dug around within myself, read books, chatted with other people, and observed life, I started connecting certain dots in my head. I can't say God often speaks as clearly to me as He did on that night (or maybe He does, and I just don't listen). But I find the more I try to see how He works, the more I see. It's about observation, patience, selflessness, and other stuff I could say that sounds wise. But mostly it's about seeing how God builds things.

Martin Smith from the band Delirious? once answered a question at a conference about what he would have done differently in his years with the group. "I wish I'd been more content with what God was doing than being so busy building my own kingdom," he said.

That struck a chord. The more I have been content to let God do His work (without having to understand or be in control or have all my plans completed), the more I have seen how amazing what He does really is. I also see how everything around me, before me, and ahead of me is one massive tapestry, all narrating His story and plan. And I love it.

What I discovered from that night forward was that I was missing some tools God had designed for me, tools I needed to do the things I could see that had to get done. And it wasn't just about a new season to pick up some new life tools; it was that I was missing them altogether. Either I didn't pick them up, or they weren't given to me, or I had them but hadn't acknowledged or learned how to use them yet.

The more I figured out the gaps in my life because of these missing tools, the more I saw what I call the Blueprint that God designed for all of us. This Blueprint has given me such clarity in life and confidence to do what He wants, even if I don't know what I am doing. The Blueprint has always existed, and it's in plain sight.

Dictionaries define a "blueprint: as a "detailed outline or plan of action." I love the definition from Collins Dictionary even more: "an original plan or prototype that influences subsequent design or practice.[1]

I want you to understand that this Blueprint for our lives is not just an idea or suggestion. Neither is it an achievement of evolving human history to refine better options or choices to create the perfect life for ourselves. The Blueprint, as I understand it, is the one God set up for the success we crave in our relationships and in our innermost being.

This book, of course, represents my perspective on that Blueprint, but the Blueprint itself is by no means my invention. I believe it was designed by God and has stood the test of time. I hope you will join me as we explore the Blueprint—and how it applies to our lives—together.

CHAPTER 1

The Blueprint Revealed

"Peter, if you want to have a band practice, you will have to go through the proper channels. I know you say you'll be careful, but if I let you do it, I'll have to let everyone else do it. I'm sorry. We can't let anyone think you get special privileges just because you're my son."

"Peter, I want you to give the gift you got at the Christmas party to that little boy over there. Yes, I know you don't want to give it, but we don't have enough gifts for everyone, so you'll have to give yours. I'll get you something else later."

"No, Peter, I don't want you telling them what you really think about them. I know they've said horrible things about us, but telling other people how bad they are just makes us look like we are as bitter as they are. I want you to say nothing."

Yes, I grew up as a pastor's kid, the youngest of four. I also grew up knowing my mum and dad as parents to more than just my siblings and me. Over the years, I saw them start a pioneering style of church; build a support network for pastors in our city, Dundee; found the first national fellowship of leaders for the many charismatic churches springing up around Scotland; and eventually travel around the world in response to the calls from far-flung churches.

In hindsight, I can see what my parents were doing was simply parenting men and women who still needed a mum and a dad. With every relationship they developed, they weren't so much building an international ministry as much as they were just making people feel safe and holding their hands as they tried to live out the sacrificial life called Christianity.

My dad was never comfortable with building an empire or a well-known ministry. He didn't even like being called "pastor." He didn't want his name emblazoned on anything and certainly didn't want to give any reason for being accused of pride. Sometimes that worked for him; sometimes it didn't. He only ever gave side hugs; he never wore jeans; he always had a comb and a handkerchief in his back pocket; and he wore old-men's aftershave every day. Being early was the only way to arrive and insisting on paying the bill was the honorable thing to do.

I loved my dad like crazy, but sometimes I felt like a victim of his high standards. Why couldn't he let me plan an event or borrow a simple piece of church equipment without going through the proper channels? Why was I the one who had to forego his Christmas present; why couldn't it be the other kid? Why did he always take the money he got from speaking at other churches and put it right into our church offering plate? Couldn't he use at least a little of it to do something nice for our family?

Because of all this and more, when God called me to pastor, I had plenty of reasons to say no. No way did I want to be anything like my dad and his sacrificial ways. Now, I'm not saying my life was terrible and my father horrible. On the contrary, I was quite privileged—I just had a lot of reasons not to go into ministry. But I quickly discovered that running from God just doesn't work. I ended up becoming a pastor in Orlando, Florida, at twenty-three years of age and have continued in ministry ever since.

So why did I finally decide to wear my father's shoes?

I did so because I felt a calling from God. And I had some emotional reasons too. Subconsciously, being a pastor somehow brought me closer to my dad. But I stayed on this path because I think I found the Blueprint my dad had in his head all along. He had been showing me (and others) all these years what it was, but at the time, I could only see the details—the blood, the sweat, and the tears.

Dad had been rebuilding what had been broken in his own house, his own city, country, and abroad. He was trying to create what I call "unscrewed-up families."

Why We Need the Blueprint

I could bemoan how society is getting worse or how much it isn't like the good old days, but I don't subscribe to that way of thinking. I don't think things were any better back then than they are today. God had a phenomenal plan and relationship structure from the beginning, and the tapestry of history has shown us how we humans—His creation, His sons, His daughters, the apples of His eye—have done things differently than He designed.

We keep repeating the same mistakes.

Whether you believe in the fall of mankind from the garden of Eden or not, anyone can see that there are times when human relationships do work, but for the most part, they are somewhat screwed up.

This is not a glass half-empty perspective; this is an admission that the glass is cracked and can't hold the water it should. Many people make an effort to pour good water into themselves and their relationships, only to discover the water doesn't remain as they expected. It leaks out. The fact that we keep trying to put good water into ourselves is testament to the resilience of the human spirit, but eventually, most people give up trying. The divorce rate alone is evidence of this.[1]

Today, we have more ways than ever to quantify our progress as humanity. We have improved our fight against disease, increased life expectancy, and created technologies to ease the effort of work. Many would argue that we have even advanced our relationship skills to be better than ever, be they parental, romantic, familial, or workplace relationships. Our riches are greater than anything our parents had. We have more now than any person or family owned in generations past.[2] But overwhelmingly, studies tell us that our happiness has not increased. Instead, it has decreased relatively.[3]

I believe in our endeavors to be both multipliers and occupiers (Gen. 1:28), and to be the conquerors we believe we are designed to be, most of us are emotionally undermined by a voice that tells us that we're not good enough after all. Every day, we see others have their dysfunctional familial relationships smeared or glossed over by the media to the point that we now call dysfunction normal. If we were fortunate enough to have our parents finally come to a place of peace with their relationships in life, should we have not left off on that same note and created better, more wholesome, and more healthful relationships? Should we not have learned from their mistakes and become wiser than they? It's like Groundhog Day; it seems we must start from the beginning all over again and go through the same cycle of dysfunction as our families of origin.

Even worse, in the name of progress, our world is reversing any semblance of what good our parents taught us to make a family great. We willfully dismantle it and come up with other family formulas. I remember my dad telling me years ago that simple mathematics tells us we will go bankrupt as a nation when we have to build twice the houses and pay twice the bills to raise one child just because two adults can't learn to live together in one house.

If the builder of the Empire State Building had to go through many lessons, mistakes, and achievements to finally end up with his masonry masterpiece, surely he could have taught his son or daughter to avoid all the mistakes he made and build an even better building with a fraction of the time, cost, and effort. Now, we have probably built better buildings, and it's reasonable to say many things in life have improved and exploded in their development since the Age of Enlightenment.

But the one area in which we have not improved, from my understanding and study, is that of the family. We haven't built better families, and we haven't risen to higher standards. And yes, we can and should do both. We should be so sick of the negative patterns and behaviors we inherited from our parents and families that we should be able to correct those problems and not repeat them. The great volume of available books and relationship advice should have helped us create marriages that last and families who live together intact.

However, the rates of increasing divorce, depression, addictions, suicides, self-harming, adults emotionally not growing up, crime rates, and more scream at us that what we're doing isn't working. I'm not going to pretend I've figured it all out or that I know exactly what a set of perfect relationships should look like, but any fool can see what doesn't work. What I see is that we have wrestled with the issue of relationships for a very long time. And we probably will keep doing so until God steps in to stop this downward cycle.

What then can we do? There is no secret formula, no snapping of the fingers to make a change. That is to say, there *is* a formula, or Blueprint, but it's not a secret. The problem is we haven't been paying attention.

I believe God has placed this Blueprint in plain sight, and as our eyes draw in to see its simplicity, I believe we finally become who we are meant to become, and any stories of dysfunctionality become mere anecdotes to our kids rather than patterns they repeat. The fact is, we can't pass on to our kids what we don't have. We can't expect them to be better than ourselves, but rather, carbon copies of ourselves. We reproduce ourselves, and any improvement is purely the grace of God.

How then can we get more of the grace of God to change what history hasn't successfully accomplished? Even better, how do we follow the steps God has already given us instead of having to constantly appeal for extra help from Him?

This book is a perspective on this Blueprint, and I hope it helps you adjust your life as you superimpose yourself on it and see where you have not been built up in accordance with its directives.

Let me warn you: This will seem too simple at first, but allow me to connect all the dots before you decide you've got it. I'll lay out the Blueprint and then show you how following its design can bring change to your life and how to have its results, its fruit, in your life.

Before We Jump In

One last thing before we jump in to examining the Blueprint itself: I am painfully aware of how easy it is to distill the answers to life's problems into a few simple concepts and leave it at that. I want to be mindful of the fact that there is a tension between the complexity and the simplicity of our problems and God's ways. Jesus had to speak in parables so we could grasp the enormity of His wisdom, which is so foreign to us.

My intention is not to dismiss the things that don't fit easily into this Blueprint perspective I am presenting. Yet neither can we allow ourselves to be immobilized by unanswered questions. I've found that this Blueprint has brought great freedom to myself and others.

Tim Keller says we commonly shrink wisdom down to three things: the physical, the psychological, and the spiritual.[4] The physical says, "All you need is medicine." The psychological says, "All you need is to talk it out and understand more." The spiritual says, "All you need is prayer," when the fact is, we need all three. They are all intertwined, and no one thing can be determined to be the root cause of issues in our lives. Physical problems can stem from psychological problems. Spiritual problems can stem from physical problems. And all vice-versa.

A more complex issue that I've found in counseling is how psychological issues like bipolar disorder can make navigating this Blueprint process more difficult. I do believe addressing family issues through the Blueprint process will always prove beneficial to the one who wants to resolve issues in their life. But the Blueprint must always be considered a partner to the other wisdom given to us, such as medication, physiotherapy, or whatever it is you need. Please don't consider changing your medication without a doctor's advice.

Finally, when Elijah was going through a mental crisis in the desert, God attended to all his needs (1 Kings 19:1-16). He fed him, let him rest, gave him solitude, and counseled him with encouragement—all before He dug into Elijah's heart to root out the spiritual issue. God attended to the whole of the person in Elijah and didn't dismiss his physical and emotional needs to tackle the spiritual. It is always better to have a mentor, a pastor, or counselor to help you walk through the reordering of your life to match the Blueprint than to try to do it alone.

Let's begin walking through the Blueprint together. I'm excited to join you in this journey.

CHAPTER 2

The Blueprint Defined

Where my eyes started to see

"Why didn't Dad ask me to come back and work for him?" I asked my mother.

This question had been gnawing at me for the seven years since my father had died of cancer in 2002. It took me that long to realize the issue troubled me, and to this day, I remember my question every time I drive that same section of road.

I didn't spring this question on my mother out of the blue. We had been talking about family matters, and the moment seemed right. Mum is a very intelligent woman and a voracious reader. A question can get an answer from her that covers so many bases and usually ends up with how God has used the Jews to be His chosen people, and we need to learn from their blessings.

An Answer—At Last

In the years since my father died, I had gone through my time of grieving and growing. Somehow telling myself Dad wasn't the first to die and wouldn't be the last gave me comfort that he hadn't carried an unfair, unshared burden and that I wasn't alone, no matter how I felt.

I learned many important lessons during this time and seemed to go through inner relationship battles that manifested themselves primarily with one person: my father-in-law, who was also my boss. I don't think it was any worse than the next man's in-law relationship, but my father-in-law demonstrated more grace and patience toward me than I realized. Maybe it was because he already saw what my dad saw about the Blueprint.

I had lived in Orlando since 1996, right around the time dad's church and ministry were starting to explode. I had wanted to be a part of that momentum, and more importantly, I wanted to serve my dad. I wanted to make him more successful. I wanted to prove that all the hard work he had done would pay off. I had spoken to him every year since and told him I was ready when he was for me to come back. And every year, he graciously thanked me but said to wait.

I didn't want to be handed his church when he died. What I wanted was to work for my dad, and I never had the chance. And what I still didn't have was a resolution to why my dad didn't want me. So my mother's answer to the question I finally asked was both pointed and life-changing: "Your dad didn't have you come to work with him because he knew you had to build your own vision and didn't want to burden you with his."

Mum may have answered the question I asked, but what I heard her say was that my dad loved me. He loved me enough to give up what he might have wanted just to give me the chance to do something fulfilling from my own hands, not his. Seven years of wondering what I should be doing weren't littered with doing nothing or being unproductive in life. No, I had helped build a church with my father-in-law, I had renovated a house with my wife, and we had started having kids. I had started my own business, traveled, and experienced many exciting things in life. But until this moment, I had been unable to see any of that. All I could see was that my dad didn't want me. And believing that lie had a huge and negative impact.

Emotionally Frozen

It's amazing how unanswered questions can stick and keep you in a time and space. I call it being emotionally frozen. It can have devastating effects on people and stunt their growth in all kinds of areas in their lives.

But for many, that stunted growth goes undetected and hides beneath what seems a perfectly normal life to anyone else. Worse, it is seemingly contradicted by what looks like success: big jobs, good money, healthy family. Only failed relationships such as problems with a spouse or children expose it.

Some years back, I was invited by some friends to a Christmas dinner party attended by mostly people I didn't know. I sat beside a retired successful criminal lawyer with whom I connected on the subjects of music and Scotland. He asked me about what I did, and I told him about my work with people through the church.

"What is the most interesting thing you have discovered in your work?" he asked.

"It's that it takes a man to teach a boy how to become a man," I said. "And if you have unresolved issues with your father, you will never properly move on from your childhood. On the inside, you're stuck there, no matter how old you get. You're emotionally frozen."

His face looked as though all the oxygen had been suddenly sucked out of the room. He slumped a little and told me how as a boy, his dad returned from Vietnam and "beat the sh__" out of him every day. In fact, he was still having nightmares about it.

Across the table, his wife was clearly uncomfortable with this conversation. "Maybe we should talk about something else," she said. She was a sitting judge at the time and may not have wanted details like these coming out about her family to some stranger. Or perhaps, subconsciously, she didn't want to see where our conversation would go. After all, it might have demanded that she face unresolved issues too. I often see this type of response.

My new friend told me he'd never heard of being emotionally frozen before but could see my answer summed up perfectly what he had struggled with since childhood. Inside, he wrestled with the conflicting memory of a father who once loved him against the memory of that same father, who mercilessly rained fists down on him. Even at seventy years old, this son was still a boy emotionally.

I tell this story to show that it matters not what age a person is. Anyone who still has unresolved parts of life is stuck, frozen. This is where we need to find out what must change to thaw out and become free.

But before we lay out the steps to do so, we must first see what is normal. What is the standard, the design, the Blueprint God has created? I also would caution at this point that you should read this entire book before deciding to apply any advice I give. I especially suggest that you find a mentor to help you apply the Blueprint to your life.

The Blueprint

The Blueprint I have discovered sets out four systematic, inviolable relationships about which we have no choice, followed by three relationships about which we do.

The relationships are as follows:

Systematic, Inviolable, Not Chosen by You: Your relationship with God, your relationship with your mother, your relationship with your father, and your relationship with your extended family (siblings, grandparents, aunts, uncles, cousins).

Flexible, Chosen by You: Your relationship with your friends, your relationship with your spouse, your relationship with your children.

CHAPTER 3

The First Four Relationships

One day, my two American brothers-in-law and I were joking about how hard our lives were since our dads were no longer around. To be clear, we know we're blessed, but we pretend our lives are harder than they are just to make light of our situations.

"My Dad wasn't around for me growing up. And I live so far away from him now it's almost like I don't have him anyway," David said in an only half-teasing tone.

"Yeah, well, I should be so lucky. At least your dad's still around. Mine's having a great time in heaven, but I don't get to talk to him much, you know?" I responded.

"You *should* be so lucky, Peter. At least you got to say goodbye to your dad. Mine dropped dead in a store of a massive heart attack," Rory told us.

Leave it to Grandma to take our banter to a whole new level. After our absent father one-upmanship, she said, "I should have been so lucky. I had five fathers, and I didn't like any of them."

Stunned, we saw the humor of the way our grandmother put each of us in our place. But we also noticed the sobering fact of her childhood experience. Growing up in the Florida Keys, Grandma did, in fact, have five father figures in her life, and hers was not a story of joy. At age nine, she nearly died in the ocean but was saved by a man who subsequently drowned saving her. She didn't have a pair of shoes until she was twelve, and her family was so poor she and her mother had to take in neighbors' laundry to survive.

Source of Life

What we may not notice in this story is that each one of us has had a mother and father; otherwise, we wouldn't have life. Regardless of how hard or how easy your life has been, you and your story would not exist unless you had a mother and a father to create you. Grandma said she had five fathers, but really, she had one father and four other father figures. Some may not have known who their parents were, but at some point, you had them, if only for a moment.

There have been actual recorded events of virgin births, but none of them except that of Mary, mother of Jesus, has produced a male human child.[1] The others have all been in the animal kingdom. It is pretty much impossible in the human realm to create a child without taking genetic material from a male and a female and combining them together, even if scientists do believe they can clone from only one person. So far, those scientists haven't created a human clone, and even if they could, it wouldn't be the norm. Nature has demanded adherence to its current process since the beginning of time, and it's worked just fine. To create a human being, there must be one male and one female.

But I believe that even before you have a mother and a father, you have been created in the mind of God. We can thus see that there is a systematic order of the relationships we have for our story of life to begin. The order of those relationships cannot change. And the first of these unchangeable relationships is with God.

Your Relationship with God

"Before I formed you in the womb I knew you, before you were born I set you apart" (Jer. 1:5b).

Trevor Yaxley was a cool Christian. Sure, he was an old man in my young teenage eyes, but his stories were wild, and he seemed to have an infectious boldness to believe in God and take big risks. Several times I had heard him speak at my father's church conferences, and in a way no one else had done, he made me believe nothing was impossible with God. Being the winner of the New Zealand 1978 Export Award for his Bubble Wrap Packaging invention[2] and then giving all of his substantial amount of money away made him immediately intriguing.

But there were a few things he said that blew my mind, especially this: "Even if you were conceived through an act of rape or lovelessness, no one can take away the fact that it took God to choose the very one sperm that fertilized your mother's egg. Out of thousands of swimmers, God reached down and allowed one specific winner to make you."

I'd never heard such a thing. Such a big finger pointing to such a little sperm. It blew my mind.

This meant we were intended. You and I were never mistakes. You were created with the participation of God Himself, regardless of how messed-up your parents may have been in the process of creating you. And no one could take that away from you. I loved this idea.

Moreover, the picture is bigger than just your human conception. God saw you in His vision, in His plan, in His Blueprint, says Jeremiah 1:5. Your beginning didn't start with the conception in the womb; it started with a conception in God's heart and mind. God saw you long before you were born.

The root word of the Hebrew word *knowledge* is "to experience or see."[3] You can't say you know something unless you have experienced it. For example, you may have heard about what Scotland is like, you may have read or seen pictures of what it's like, but until you have been there and experienced it, you simply don't know it. And yet, somehow, before you even existed in the flesh, God knew you. It's as though He literally experienced you in His plan, His vision of you.

To take this further, even the word *conceive* is applied to our understanding of vision as much as it is to join a sperm to an egg. "I conceived a great idea," you may say. The conception of what that idea is exists before its actual physical reality. God always conceived and shared His ideas long before He brought them into actual physical existence. He shared great visions with our forefathers far ahead of the time when the actual events came to pass.

No doubt, He talked endlessly with Adam and Eve about the cool things He wanted to help them discover and create. He showed Jacob a vision of how a nation would be born through him. And when it came to the idea of you, He spoke and conceived your person long before you were ever brought to pass.

"This is all very nice, Peter. But really! Isn't this just conjecture of cheer and comfort? Does God really point to one sperm?"

Well, let's see.

How God Tied Himself to You

I spoke at a conference called Sex Matters a few years ago, and I was tasked with teaching about the plan of God in sex. During my studies, I kept having this nagging statement stick in my head: "It's a covenant."

Of course, that sounded lofty enough, and at least if I said it, no one could argue with me much about its "truthiness" or relevance, especially since this was a Christian conference. But it just felt too vague. I felt like God was poking me to go find out what covenant really meant in this context. So, after study and research, I landed on a revelation about this that went way deeper than I had ever discovered before.

The four points were that sex was about offspring (kids), orgasm (the fun of it), oath (covenant), and order. The first two points I will assume you understand. The last two are closely tied together.

Every time God made an oath (a covenant), he always accompanied it with a specific order of how the blessing should be procured or experienced.[4] And every time there was order, it seemed to have been preceded by some pronunciation of a covenant. The Bible contains many examples of covenants and orders, but the most significant one, which shows how God makes this work, was God's covenant with Abram (Gen. 15).

Since it all went wrong at the beginning with Adam and Eve, Abram was the man God chose to create a covenant of restoration between humankind and Himself. Abram's was the first covenant—culminating in Jesus dying on a cross—to bring this great plan to pass, but the steps of his original covenant are a little perplexing.

Now let me make this clear. Here is how I understand the meaning of *covenant* as I have studied it:

Dictionary meaning: "a commitment to future behavior.[5]

Strong's Concordance, Hebrew - 1285, 1262, 1254 meaning: "To selectively create by passing between pieces of flesh."[6]

The meaning derived from Strong's is odd, and I had to do more study and research to understand it. The Hebrew meaning is based on several words that all seem to be connected and don't stand alone to hold the only meaning of the word. A better Hebrew scholar would be able to expound on this for us, but a revelation came to me when

I saw how God made his covenant with Abram. His promise to make offspring for the father of Israel seemed to match the way He designed Adam and Eve to wield the creative force of conceiving a child.

In Genesis 15, Abram asks God how he will know that God will really give him children as He had declared. Abram is essentially asking, "How will I know You are committed to this future action of creating children through me?" (Remember the dictionary meaning of the word *covenant*).

God answered by ordering a selection of animals to be brought and told Abram to cut each animal in two. He then put Abram into a deep sleep (much as He did with Adam when He created Eve), and then a smoking firepot with a blazing torch appeared and passed between the pieces of animal carcasses.

God was acting out what His part would be in the process of this covenant: He would pass between two pieces of flesh and create something. In the same way, I believe God's creative power and presence pass between a man and a woman (two pieces of flesh) when they are having intercourse. Right in that moment, His covenant, which allows us to be like Him in creating another human, is enacted. His commitment to the future behavior of making another person is invoked, and He selectively chooses which sperm will fertilize the egg. His covenant is there between two pieces of flesh, namely, your mum and your dad.

Do you see how God knew you, intended you, and created you even as your parents chose or did not chose to be a part of the process? Think about it: Why didn't God empower us to create offspring by the two ways He created things Himself? He created by speaking creation into being, and He also created by forming Adam out of soil.

I believe that apart from our sexual relationship, which requires the involvement of both a male and a female, God designed procreation this way so He would always be involved as well. In other words, you can't exist without God first knowing you, having conceived you in His plan and vision, and being actively involved in your physical manifestation in the world.

God knew you before you were born, and your relationship with Him is the first one you have, whether you remember it or not. We'll return to this point later, since in the end, everything loops back around to this essential relationship.

Your Relationship with Your Mother

"She shall be called wombed-man," (Gen. 2:23b).

Thank God we don't remember the trauma it must be to squeeze down the birth canal. My sister Catriona is a midwife and is often scheduled on call by herself at a small birth unit in a town somewhere in Scotland. In the middle of the night, a ready-to-burst pregnant mother arrives, and Catriona jumps into action to guide the process.

I admit, I don't think I could do what my sister does. Her stories are too crazy and stressful for me. For that matter, I don't think I could do what women do in giving birth. Thank God for midwives and women who bring us into this world.

When God created woman, the one major difference between her and man was the fact that she has a womb to carry and incubate a child. Hence the name *wombed-man*, now shortened to *woman*.

You don't remember that incubation and probably don't remember the first years of your life, when you depended on your mother for intense physical nurture. Without our mother's care, we wouldn't survive. From the moment of conception, we are 100 percent dependent on our mothers until we can feed ourselves or be fed by someone else. But at that stage, we need more than just physical sustenance. There is also a spiritual dependence that we may acknowledge but likely undervalue.

Normal Mother-Child Relationship

According to the Blueprint, it's normal that as you grow as a child, you should have the experience of being mothered. Not smothered, but rather, cared for in only the way a mother can do. There is a tenderness that should come from your mother even if she has a firm hand to direct you at the same time. Children usually run to their mother for comfort when they are injured, and science indicates that infants are drawn to the higher voice tones their mothers emit.[7]

You may have noticed how people's voices naturally go to the higher range when speaking to a baby. Women have this higher range naturally built in, compared to the lower male vocal range. This is not to say your mother's voice is what determines a normal relationship with her, but it is evidence of the natural affinity a mother has to make a connection with her child, hers being the first human relationship a child has.

I won't argue against questions about different personalities, tough mothers, stay-at-home dads, and so forth. It's a well-known fact that mothers generally provide this first human relationship, and I see every day that it's usual for a child to receive tenderness, sustenance, and protection *first* from their mother, starting in the womb. That's normal.

Though we may not mentally register it, I believe we are also affected by what our mother feels when we are in the womb. If your mother was depressed or happy, you felt it. This continued into early childhood; whatever your mother experienced rubbed off on you, maybe not so much as a cognitive registering but as an emotional one. What she felt, you felt.

Here's what my wife, Crystal, has to say about this stage:

I found out I was pregnant with our first child, Cael, on the morning after I had been out with some old friends, enjoying a few alcoholic drinks. Nothing says, "Welcome to motherhood" like the nagging feeling of instantaneous guilt. And at the initial visit with my obstetrician a few weeks later, I learned that apparently, the small amount of alcohol consumed that night couldn't hold a candle to the other toxins I had been eating: luncheon meats, sushi, seafood (I was craving and eating an amount of tuna that would make an orca blush). The doctor also warned me that pregnancy can make even a common cold feel much worse, since cold medicine is on the forbidden list too. I'm sure I was pale as I walked out of my obstetrician's office after that first visit. *This kid is doomed!* I thought.

There are many differing opinions on what can and cannot be consumed during pregnancy and admittedly, I was a bit laxer with my second. However, it is agreed both universally and scientifically that whatever you eat, the baby eats. Your eating habits have a direct effect on baby, whether positive or negative. In the same way, your emotions have a direct effect on baby, whether positive or negative.

Often, as mothers, we pay close attention and put much emphasis on what we are eating and the state of our physical health in pregnancy; however, we place little emphasis and time on building and strengthening our emotional health. Unfortunately, it is often not until years later that we realize how much our feelings while pregnant affected our unborn children.

Your Relationship with Your Father

"Fathers, do not exasperate your children; instead, bring them up in the training and instruction of the Lord" (Eph. 6:4).

My father was an engineer before he was a pastor. He followed in his father's footsteps and designed the engines and mechanics for ships, most famously working on the drawings and designs for the engines of HMS *Queen Elizabeth II* (the QE2). Giving instructions was his thing. He wasn't much of a right-brain, artistic-type thinker but most definitely a left-brain, analytical, instructive type thinker. And your father may have been completely and wonderfully different.

Normal Father-Child Relationship

A normal relationship as shown by the Blueprint finds your connection to your father growing after the immediate and intimate relationship you have with your mother. You're inside your mum, and there's a barrier between you and your dad. Even in infancy, the initial order of food source is usually from your mother's body. Gradually, your relationship with your father builds as he co-parents to give you instruction for life.

Ultimately, this instruction is for the purpose of making you a whole human being—physically, emotionally, and mentally balanced. The goal here is to safeguard your life, enabling you to live it out well and pass on everything good to the next generation.

Statistics abound on the importance of a present father in a child's life.[8] The increased likelihood of young teenagers being sexually active linked to the lack of an involved father in their lives is no coincidence. A father protects and sets standards a child should want to attain. These protection-standards are not for the child to perform to match some prior prudish cultural norms. Instead, they're in place so the child can gain safety from predators, the ability to make good choices, the confidence to take risks and improve, the inquisitiveness to stretch safe boundaries and run from dangerous ones, the grit to push through challenges, a balanced perspective that some things matter and other things don't, and most importantly, the ability to grow emotionally into normal, functional adulthood. All these are marks of a normal father-child relationship.

John Eldredge's *Fathered by God* [9] is an essential book that I believe every man should read. It lays out the clearest pattern of stages a male goes through from boyhood to manhood. His insight on how each stage must be acknowledged and fulfilled is much like the Blueprint I am presenting, but he focuses only on men. Eldredge examines the need for boys to go through two specific stages with a father's guidance: *boyhood* and *cowboy*.

I loved his description of these stages; you can tell a book's impact by the picture it leaves in your mind. The picture that immediately jumps to my attention for these two stages is of a boy being kissed on the head by his dad, and then of the dad challenging his son to ride his bike just a little farther down the road from his house, thus pushing his boundaries.

Eldredge's *boyhood* stage, which we'll call the *childhood* stage, identifies a child being loved by his dad. A father does more than instruct a child for good. He balances it with unconditional acceptance at the other end of the scale, regardless of how well or poorly the child has responded to the instruction. I say "at the other end of the scale" because in between is the father's challenge to the child to push himself, his support during the pushing, his recognition of the little achievements his child has made, and his ending it all with kisses on the child's head. That's a normal relationship between father and child.

The *cowboy* stage, which we'll call the *adventurer* stage, finds a child being shown how to push the boundaries in life in a calculated risk, as-safe-as-possible-but-throwing-some-caution-to-the-wind kind of way.

As important as a good schedule and a clear structure are in life, those boundaries should be interspersed with "Kids! Let's do something crazy." Of course, I don't mean crazy at the expense of the child's life, education, safety, or future. I mean a dad eating ice cream with his kids before dinner—just because it's Saturday. I mean letting the daughter paint her dad's nails because it's funny. I mean a dad who knows how to make a child study harder, try new ventures, serve others first, get away from the TV, try something new, or stick with a chore—and all the while, chooses to have fun at it.

Carlos, a friend of mine, is a great dad. He expected high moral standards, behavior, and work ethics from his son, and he knew how to make a moment happen to instill the adventurer into him. One day, he pulled out a map on the kitchen table and opened his laptop to the local airport flight schedule. He told his son, "Let's do something crazy. Pick a city! Where do you want to go?"

His son, beaming and asking whether his dad was "for real," picked a city, and the two matched it up to a flight leaving that day. They caught the plane and, a few hours later, landed in the city the son had chosen. What were they going to do? It didn't matter; they were already doing it. They were having an adventure.

The adventure didn't have to cost money. It didn't have to take them to another city. It just had to be an adventure.

This is the Blueprint's version of a normal relationship of a child with a father, meaning the dad is present in the child's life to instruct, challenge, cheer, and love his child.

Your Relationship with Your Extended Family

"A good person leaves an inheritance for their children's children" (Prov. 13:22a).

It was seven o'clock in the morning, and I could hear the rain dropping on the roof of our four-berth camper trailer that was not designed for a family of six. The sound of the wind alone let us know it was cold outside, something to be expected at Stonehaven campground by the North Sea in a land notorious for its dearth of sunshine. The phrase "You know it's summer in Scotland because the rain is warmer" is both levity and reality.

My brother, the firstborn, nudged me awake and asked if I wanted to come with him into the village to get some milk for the family. I said no, probably because my corner of the camper was far more inviting than launching out into the rain. And providing him companionship or serving the family by making a milk run didn't enter my five-year-old mind.

"I'll buy you a Milky Way," he said.

"OK."

And just like that, I was out of bed and pullin' ma clae's awn (pulling my clothes on). Oh, what powers a sweet chocolate treat can wield over a child.

My brother was always generous like that. No, not with the Milky Ways (though he was) but with getting the milk for everyone. It's a very firstborn thing: be responsible, be a provider, look five steps ahead to minimize future effort and maximize results.

My sisters, too, have very telling characteristics that seem to follow their birth order. Catriona, offspring number two, is very much a middle child and likes to make sure everyone feels special. To her, no one should feel left out, which is why she is very generous when it comes to giving gifts. She can recall anyone's birthday and has never missed recognizing someone's special day—at least in our family. Fiona, offspring number three, is the people organizer, a let's-have-fun, why-are-we-sitting-here type. She doesn't take no for an answer, because boring doesn't give life the respect it deserves. We should go out and conquer it every day!

Your extended family consists of your siblings, aunts, uncles, cousins, and grandparents. You have no control over the existence of these relationships; they are chosen for you. However, they may not exist in any form of physical interaction. You may have none of these. You may be the only child of only children, but you most definitely had or have grandparents. Mine died when I was two years old. I don't remember them and always felt a little jealous of my friends who had theirs around. But we all at least had grandparents, an extended family.

You are positioned somewhere in your family according to your birth order. The picture I've painted of mine is in no way the norm. Different sizes, different age gaps, different genders, and so on make up all kinds of different families. But one thing all families have in common is some form of relationship, healthy or not. And those relationships are forged through understanding how to respond to the individuals' different personalities and negotiating the depths of those relationships.

Maybe you connect with one extended family member more than another. Maybe it's because they are nice to you. Maybe it's because they get your jokes. Maybe it's like-mindedness, age, vicinity, or something else. But in every relationship, you are learning how to interact with the wider world first through your interactions with your extended family, their personalities, and their choices in life.

Teachers, Babysitters, and Other People

Your mother and your father cannot give you every tool for life. We learn so many different things from different sources, but we primarily take our lead from our parents and then our wider family.

"Wow, you are so like your nephew." I don't know how many times I've heard this statement from young girls fawning over my teenage nephews,

No. My nephews are so like me. I came first; they came later. I understand they're not really interested in my correction of the birth order, but it is true that my nephews have probably been affected by the way I act and talk.

Let's consider other influences, though, ones we don't necessarily choose like teachers, babysitters, and other authorities. Do they not fit into this Blueprint order? Yes and no.

Teachers, babysitters, and similar figures are only in your life because your mother, father, and extended family have generally chosen to allow them there. They may have power and influence over you, but they did not acquire this by their own choice alone. It's usually by permission of the primary guardians, namely, your family. This is why, even if you have been hurt by a teacher or babysitter, you must first deal with the fact that the hurt only came into your life through the permission or oversight of a family member.

Often, you don't realize the existence of an emotional attribution of blame toward your dad because something did or didn't happen to you, even if he had no intention of it occurring. Why? Because it's his job to protect you and provide for you. Unfortunately, our parents can't cover every base in our lives.

Thus, we see that it's normal to have relationships with people outside our extended family, but they only exist because our father, mother, and extended family allow them.

We'll move on to some other vital relationships in the next chapter.

CHAPTER 4

The Last Three Relationships

The relationships you do choose

A baked potato and my friend Jimmy Marshal were the only things I wanted for my sixth birthday. That's all! No birthday cake. No special games. No Pin the Tail on the Donkey. No streamers. No presents or banners. Just a baked potato and Jimmy Marshal.

My mother was probably quietly pleased that I had asked for so little for the big day. She wouldn't need to corral twenty-five screaming children high on birthday cake to keep them from destroying her house. She wouldn't need to negotiate for a lesser event that would be appropriate to her budget. She wouldn't have to explain why I couldn't have the latest toy that was for ages ten and older. I just wanted a baked potato and Jimmy Marshal.

Best Friends

Why did I ask for so little? Maybe it was my personality—I appreciate more the company of a few good friends over a roomful of acquaintances—but I think it was that I'd never had a best friend before.

Jimmy Marshal was the kid I immediately connected with when I first attended school. His dad owned a newspaper shop at the top of my road, and I thought that was so cool. Jimmy got to read all the comics without having to pay for any of them. His dad had a brand-new car. and when he took us to school in it, I felt like we were kings being dropped off in a limousine.

Jimmy was my best friend. Jimmy was the first and only person on my list of invited guests to my sixth birthday party. Jimmy was my best friend—did I say that already?

Most anyone will remember their first best friend, even if the friendship doesn't last for a lifetime as you promised it would. No one usually needs to teach you about how a best-friend relationship works or how to long for one. It just kind of happens. You meet someone you click with, maybe you verbally agree that this mutual status is now written in stone, and you relate to each other in a manner that is elevated in a special way above all other relationships. You have chosen someone for a special relationship, and they have chosen you.

This best-friendship represents the first relationship that wasn't chosen for you. This type of relationship is part of the last three relationships, which you have a major part in choosing. These are the ones you have with your friends, your spouse, and your children. These are relationships you don't have to have, and we don't necessarily always place them in the order I've listed. Although you don't have to have any of these, most people choose to have at least one of them. I haven't included work colleagues or in-laws because they are secondary to the impact these next three relationships have on you.

Let me again clarify that these relationships don't necessarily follow in the order I am presenting, but it seems more the norm that they do and should. First, any of us who has a best friend treasures the camaraderie that comes from that relationship, but it shouldn't supersede the intimate relationship of a spouse. And the best-friend relationship is ready to exist long before you're ready to go find a spouse.

Second, trying to build that depth of friendship with a friend other than your spouse is a lot harder to do once you're married when you should be attending to the relationship with your spouse. It's not impossible; it's just harder. I could combine my best friend and my spouse as one person (and eventually you should), but usually a person has a best-friend relationship with someone of the same sex first and then marries someone of the opposite sex. It's beyond the scope of this book to discuss same-sex couples or having a best friend of the opposite sex. I don't believe that same-sex marriage is in keeping with God's Blueprint because a marriage is for more than just companionship or personal compatibility. I believe marriage is for creating and raising children, who also need a mother and a father in their lives and are best served with that mother and father living in a mutually beneficial relationship we call marriage.

Having a best friend of the opposite sex (even without romance) can also create problems. Those issues can make for great movie storylines, but I've had many friends who have had to distance themselves from their opposite-sex best friend when they got married because their new spouse didn't appreciate them having a competing intimate relationship with someone of the opposite sex.

Maybe you have questions about whether I am right or wrong on these two issues I've mentioned. Maybe you disagree with my logic. I am speaking both generally and specifically here but don't have the room in this book to delve deeper into an explanation of my position. At this point, even if you disagree, please accept that I don't believe it's part of God's Blueprint.

In the same way, having children before you have a spouse doesn't stand the test of reality that says it's not the best order. This is not to diminish the exemplary efforts of single parents who fight to give their children the best that they can, but there is too much available science and evidence to prove that a functional two-parent upbringing is far better for a child than a one-parent environment. [1] A Blueprint match? No!

So let's look at the last three relationships in your life.

Your Relationship with Your Friends

"Do not be misled: 'Bad company corrupts good character'" (1 Cor. 15:33).

"Wounds from a friend can be trusted" (Prov. 27:6a).

Growing up, from age twelve on, Craig was my best friend. I had other best friends, but I discovered they were only so in name only. Craig was my real best friend. Yes, we hung out together. Yes, we got on famously and experienced many male-bonding adventures together, but it was more than that. I always felt like he "got me" the most. He completed so many areas of my life. We didn't like or want the same things, but there were certain things I wanted or needed that he helped me with, and I gave to him in the areas he needed as well.

I was never good with the ladies. If I liked a girl, I couldn't be myself with her. I was stoic. I'd avoid her, or I'd bombard her in what I thought was witty humor but ended up just being sarcasm. Somehow, I ended up giving her anything other than the impression that I liked her.

But Craig. Craig! He was way smoother than I. And I don't mean in a manipulative, creepy, or disrespectful way. He just knew how to make a girl laugh or feel special. She always got the message, and she always seemed to be flattered that he liked her. Yes, he was a good-looking guy, but I saw ugly guys get the same results, so I couldn't put his advantage down to appearance. He had a skill I didn't, and I never flew at his level. But he helped me to remove unnecessary stumbling blocks such as not believing a girl could ever like me. I had big insecurities, and he was a peer voice I could trust, even if it was to critique.

Another way Craig and I connected was that he always felt his mind was inadequate. He was a person with dyslexia, and I did well at most academic pursuits. He had to work harder than everyone else just to get passing grades, but I think I brought him confidence. Yes, he should work hard. No, it didn't matter how well he wrote. I believe I treated him with the respect of being an equal that didn't discount his value based on his learning abilities, and our mutual encouragement deepened. Craig is now a very successful emergency-response rescuer who flies in an air ambulance helicopter all over the U.K. to the worst of emergency scenarios. Not bad for a guy with dyslexia.

What Craig and I did was help each other. No wonder he was my best friend.

Good, Better, Best

You have so many different types of friends, and those circles shrink in their emotional nearness to you in the order of good, better, and best. They also shrink in number from being many, to fewer, and few. I think Jesus had these circles too.

Good

Jesus had about sixty disciples, possibly more—including women—in the group who followed him for a while (Luke 10). He helped them, and they helped him. But when it came to His challenge through a teaching about drinking His blood and eating His flesh, they found the limitation of their friendship with Him (John 6:53-60). They weren't bad people, and I don't think they stopped being friends, but their trust, commitment, and reliability weren't forged deep enough at that point.

Note this: When they left Him, He didn't criticize them or seem hurt, because He no doubt understood their boundaries. You can easily lose the close proximity of friendship with this type of friend if you spill too much of your emotions, personal information, or vision on them. Don't be surprised if they back away from you when you become challenging. I don't think the actions of His friends surprised Jesus at all.

Better

The next group of friends Jesus had was His eleven disciples (I'll assume Judas is a separate case). They distinguished themselves as the ones who truly bought into the vision of His life—but not because they actually understood that vision. The fact that they didn't leave Him when the other sixty or so did was more out of blind zeal than noble commitment. They basically said, "We don't get his weird teaching, but we have no Plan B, so let's see where this leads."

I really value these types of people around me, because they go through thick and thin with me, and yet I'm never sure they understand me. They just love me and stay with me. The good friends and the better friends seem very much alike, but the glaring difference is that the latter stay with you. What a treasure. They stay!

Best

The final group of friends is the best friends. If you can have at least one, you are a wealthy person. Jesus had three: Peter, James, and John. He symbolically showed Himself completely to them when He transfigured before them on a mountain (Matt. 17:1-13). He literally showed them His glory and was completely transparent before them about who He really was. Showing people this much of yourself requires a lot of trust, because the rejection and the ridicule that could follow would be crushing.

We might imagine that Jesus' inner strength was such that He never felt vulnerable or rejected by His family or friends, but I would beg to differ. He was still human. He felt it when his friends couldn't stay awake praying for Him in the Garden of Gethsemane, and I'm sure He could have felt it in all the other times he was vulnerable with them.

But this is one of the greatest joys of having a best friend. When you are weak, you can truly lean on them. When you are happy, you can be truly childlike with them. You can share yourself across the entire range of emotions. That's a best friend.

Your Relationship with Your Spouse

"The Lord God said, 'It is not good for the man to be alone. I will make a helper suitable for him'" (Gen. 2:18).

But for Adam no suitable helper was found. So the LORD God caused the man to fall into a deep sleep; and while he was sleeping, he took one of the man's ribs and then closed the place with flesh. Then the LORD God made a woman from the rib he had taken out of the man, and he brought her to the man.

The man said, 'This is now bone of my bones and flesh of my flesh; she shall be called "woman," for she was taken out of man.'

That is why a man leaves his father and his mother and is united to his wife, and the two shall become one flesh (Matt. 2:18-25).

This passage is the first time God ever said something wasn't good: Adam by himself was not a good thing. It seems odd that God would make such a statement. He couldn't have made a mistake. But how could something be missing? God makes all things perfect.

Adam's design and existence weren't wrong or imperfect. He had been designed in God's image, and God had a deep desire to love and share what He had. What Adam was missing was the ability to love and share what he had with someone else like himself. I love this reality, because it means you are no less a person if you don't have a spouse. Instead, it means your God-design gives you a deep desire to share what you find, make, and experience. That's normal.

One of the coolest things God did was to invent a relationship one level above a best friend. What he essentially did was to split Adam in two and allow each half to complete the other. This is why God says two become one (Gen. 2:24) when they are in covenant with each other. Eve was originally inside Adam, and God removed the female part. Eve was never second or an afterthought; she was always there. Initially, the name "Adam" is neither a male or a female name.[2] He only became completely male after his Eve side was removed.

A Good Relationship with a Good Mate

I think a bright green dress was my defibrillator in finding my spouse. I had known Crystal for a couple of years. I worked for her dad and lived with her grandmother, but we didn't necessarily click. We are both pastor's kids, and neither of us wanted to marry one. She had her strong opinions and apparently, so did I. These reasons alone were enough to make us rub each other the wrong way.

But something happened on that sunny Florida day by the lake with her extended family. I went through the drowsy wake-up experience I think Adam also experienced. Everything really does go into slow motion the way it does in the movies, at least in my memory. I wasn't ready to really like her, but bam! I didn't have a choice. Seeing her in that bright green dress was my Adam moment.

"Bone of my bones, flesh of my flesh" (Gen. 2:23b), Adam said. I don't really know what he was going on about, but I think he was trying to say, "Woooow!" At least, that's the way I interpreted it in that moment by the lake.

It wasn't really Crystal's dress or her obvious beauty. It was a culmination of knowing her over time, becoming good friends, and realizing she was a perfect match for me in so many ways. My brain connected all the dots in that moment, and now I had to weigh up what this meant and decide if the pursuit was on.

I'm not going to say that this Adam-seeing-Eve revelation will happen the same way for you. I can't say what is the right or wrong way to meet the one who makes all your senses explode. I'm not going to pretend that there isn't more than one person who has sparked that thrill in you. I'm not even going to say you can't pursue someone with whom you don't have that huge "wow" feeling, or, to this point, that you wouldn't have second guesses about the person after a "wow" feeling.

But let's be honest. These are more problems with your maturity, your ability to understand your emotions, to wait or not wait, to properly weigh up the pros and cons, to choose, to commit, and to have proper expectations of love. God hasn't made a perfect match for you with one person. If that were true, then you marrying the wrong person would mean the person they were meant to marry has to marry another wrong person and so on, setting off an infinite array of wrong matches for everyone.

The Blueprint is what God has made perfect. He's made a perfect way for you to be matched to one of the best options to whom He can so ably lead you. There is a reason He has placed all the relationships leading up to this big spouse-step first, because they prepare you and build you up to readiness.

There are so many categories to consider when weighing up a match, including personalities, life goals, personal ethics and faith, intentions for provision, child-rearing, and so on. It is normal to depend on your parents, your family, and your friends to help you wisely choose a mate. That wisdom can come in the form of live advice on the end of a phone or sage wisdom planted in you from past family and friend relationships. All along, others should be placing tools in your life to be able to make wise choices like choosing a mate. That is a normal part of the Blueprint.

Your Relationship with Your Children

"Children are a heritage from the LORD, offspring a reward from him" (Ps. 127:3).

When the ultrasound technician asked if we wanted to know, we said yes.

"Well, it's a girl!"

I jumped out of my chair and started hopping around, shouting and laughing. "Woohooo, yes, yes, yes." Rowan is our second child, born after our son, Cael, and I seriously would have been the same crazy-happy if she had been a boy. But regardless, it just felt great hearing whom we were expecting.

The only sad news I walked away with that day was a statement the ultrasound technician made that has stuck in my brain.

"I'm glad you're happy," she told me.

"Yeah, this is awesome!"

"I've been doing this for over twenty years, and I've never seen a father be demonstrably happy like that on hearing it was a girl," she said. "Only when it's been a boy."

If you are a parent and you didn't feel the same excitement about having a girl as I did, you have to be out of your mind. Even if the joy was lacking when you had a boy, it's not normal. Psalm 127:3 tells us children are a gift from God. A gift. From God!

Equal Joy

The joy of having a child is one that should be set up to benefit you and the child equally. I say "equally" because again, the relationships prior to this childbearing step are meant both to prepare you to enjoy your children and to prepare your children to enjoy you.

Based on the readiness of your emotions, finances, home life, and spousal relationship, having children is a normal "next step." My experience is that in most cases, the lack of readiness we may have is due to our own poor choices. In a normal, healthy spousal relationship, there are few times a child's conception and birth are completely out of our control. Even in those times when, say, the contraception didn't work, an unexpected pregnancy does not change our responsibility to receive this child with joy.

Let me say at this point that I sympathize deeply with those who wish to have children but can't. I have both family and close friends who have experienced this situation, and I wouldn't venture to say that I understand. This particular scenario is outside the scope of this book, but please know I acknowledge that some steps that seem so normal for most of us are very painful for many others who can't take that step. My heart is with you.

I was the fourth child and unplanned, but my parents, even with the few resources they had, received me with all the effort and reception any child deserves. In plain English: You should not be having sex with the potential of having a child if you have not first prepared your life to receive a child, should it happen. It is only fair to the child to welcome them into a marriage and environment prepared to receive them and nurture them in every way.

But the joy belongs equally to the child. You could be as ecstatic, ready to receive and raise that child as anyone else, but if you have not put the effort in to provide them with the best chance of following the Blueprint, you cheat your child. God has designed the Blueprint so your child's life should be set up to have the same joy that comes from it as you do. Of course, I'm referring to having a mum and dad ready for your child in a loving, intact marriage and household (scenarios like parental death aside). It's normal for your child to expect this opportunity.

Your Child's Future in Your Choices

Bruce's marriage was crashing and had been for some time.

"My wife's too controlling," he told me. "I fear for my kids' lives if they're left alone with her. She's abusive."

Whether his statements were true or not, there was little he could do. After all, she was their mother and had every right to be in their lives (aside from proven abuse, in which case law enforcement should be called).

"How did you meet? How did you end up deciding to marry her?"

He shared the story of a rapid courtship. "The first clue I had of her extreme control was on our wedding day. Nothing I did was good enough. When it came to making decisions that we both should have made she arbitrarily made them all without consulting me. I had no say in anything. And it's been that way ever since."

"Why didn't you halt things right there?"

"I figured she'd change once we got married."

"Well, did her control issues subside by the time you had your first child?"

"No way. That came several years later, but no way. She was worse—a lot worse."

"May I ask a question? If you knew she was so much worse, why did you decide to have a child at all?"

"I don't know. I guess I thought my love—and becoming a mother—would soften her somehow."

"You had your second child a few years later. Had your wife improved by then?"

"Nope, she was even worse."

At that point I had to ask an even harder question. "If your wife is as bad as you say she is, who gave you the right to burden your children with such an awful mother? You say you saw how bad she was all along, yet you kept taking the risk of having a broken marriage and an abusive mother for your children."

I continued, "You are laying all the burden at her feet. Either you're looking for an excuse to leave your wife, or you gave your kids a horrible mother, and you're not taking responsibility for your part in that. Whatever your answer is, your kids lose."

Here's the issue: All of our choices as to how we respond to the Blueprint God has given us end up as a benefit or a burden to our children. And our choices either set them up to repeat our success or our failures. Usually, they follow our pattern. Yes, good parents can have bad kids, but that's not the norm. And yes, a great kid can come from a bad parent, but that kid has to work hard to correct the bad-behavior model they've received. Statistics and studies are overwhelmingly in favor of a child being raised with a mum and a dad in a marriage together.[3]

I have to agree with radio host Dr. Laura Schlessinger when she says that the reason we don't see the red flags of a bad relationship with a future mate is because we don't *want* to see them.[4] Many people that I have counseled over the years believed the only reason they weren't able to provide a guaranteed father or mother for their child rested on the fact that their spouse left, which was outside of their control. However, it helps to see that there were often red flags indicating that their potential mate was not the best choice for them or for their future children. Knowing how to spot those red flags would help us to make more informed choices when it comes to future relationships. I understand that due to young age, inexperience, or lack of outside input, we can't always see the signs, and sometimes a person who started out wonderful can turn into a difficult person later in life. But imagine if we could see those red flags and make much better choices.

You may say, "How could I have known for sure my spouse wouldn't be a good dad? Again, the answer lies in the Blueprint. God has set it up for your success when you follow it.

Even the famous Dr. Phil McGraw concurs that it's a rare case where there weren't any red flags.[5] And if you were not afforded the Blueprint of great parents and a wonderful extended family to teach you how to spot those red flags, then the onus is on you to resolves your issues, learn, and get the tools you need *before* you decide to launch your kids on the journey of their Blueprint. Ultimately, it will be your children who will pay the price for your emotional dysfunctionality or benefit from your emotional strength.

Please note a problem I have encountered multiple times with people I have counselled over the years. When I ask them to tell me about their first four relationships, they are honest enough to answer my questions and reveal where their upbringing did not match the

Blueprint. However, they will often tell me how wonderful their father or mother was and gloss over any dysfunctionality.

Tom and his wife came to see me because their communication and marriage were deteriorating. After some talk about their marriage and the problems they were experiencing, I asked Tom about his first four relationships. He had a very secure upbringing with siblings, a stay-at-home mother who nurtured them as best she could, and a father who worked hard and paid the bills.

"Tom, tell me what a typical day was like in your home."

"Well, it was a normal household. My mom would wake us up in the morning and get us ready for school. I was the middle boy of three, and we were pretty rambunctious. Mom would send us off to school and she would stay home looking after the house. Then at the end of the school day we'd stop off at the dime store and get some candy and head on home."

"What would happen when you got home?"

"You know! Same old stuff. We'd do our homework, play outside, get dinner, play some more, and then head off to bed to start the whole day over again."

Everything seemed normal.

"Where was your dad in the story, Tom?"

"Well, he was at work."

"At work? All day."

"Yeah. He'd leave before us and would get back after we were in bed. He worked in a city far away, and his commute was pretty long. So we never saw him as much. He was a pretty hard worker."

After talking further, I realized that during Tom's childhood, his father worked so much that he rarely spent time with his son. Tom couldn't see that this was a problem. But then I made the connection for him:

"Tom, I want to suggest that the reason you are struggling to communicate with your wife is because you never saw your father properly communicate with your mother. Your dad was never around, so you never saw your parents resolve problems together. You never learned the skills your father should have taught you."

In other words, his dad didn't demonstrate this part of the Blueprint.

It's natural for people to gloss over the quiet dysfunctional parts of their family if they have never properly known the Blueprint. How can they know? How could Tom admit that his dad failed him if he didn't know that the Blueprint includes a father and mother who demonstrate normal communication and problem-solving skills in their marriage?

This is why this and the previous chapter are essential. We must understand how these seven relationships were designed to function.

Now that we have an overview of the Blueprint, we are ready to examine how to correct it if your life, superimposed over the top of it, doesn't match in places. The good news is that you can find resolution for the missing parts in your Blueprint. You can move forward, and you can set your kids up for success. In the rest of the book, we will investigate how we can do this appropriately.

CHAPTER 5

The First Half Affects the Second Half

Martin grew up with little direction from his parents about how to handle money. He said he was always in financial trouble, so I asked him to write down every penny that came in and every penny that went out.

After a few weeks, we had a small picture of how he spent his money. I noticed the first thing he did was to cash his check at a cash-checking store that charged him ten percent for the service. "Why don't you have a bank account? That way, you wouldn't have to pay to cash your checks."

"I don't like banks," he told me.

He must be hiding something–a legal or financial issue that makes him want to avoid banks, I thought. But with further probing, I realized this wasn't the case. He was just scared of the idea of using a bank. It intimidated him.

God intended that Martin's parents teach him how to handle money and banks. But because they didn't give him the right tools, he had instead picked up their tool of suspicion and fear of banks and was applying this replacement tool to his financial life. His replacement tool had worked up to this point, but he was losing ten percent every time he received a paycheck. Now, his tool was working against him. His emotions didn't let him choose the better way of cashing his checks. He didn't even respond enthusiastically when I said I could help him stop losing ten percent of his money.

Let's start by acknowledging that we are not in a perfect world, and we have all received good and bad things from our past relationships. Maybe you have had a good mum and dad and don't see any negative effects on yourself. Yet, you can still have inner blockages and frustrations you can't seem to overcome. You can't pinpoint their source. This is why we consider the Blueprint first—because we can't see all the things we need to address without a map to guide us. This isn't about trying to fix all past relationships but about moving you forward to become what you were designed to be and to set your kids up for success.

Your first four relationships (God, mother, father, extended family) affect your last three relationships (friends, spouse, kids). Your ability to choose good relationships in the latter is fully influenced by the relationships you didn't choose in the former. The first half affects the second half.

And so, this first half affects three distinct abilities: the ability to choose, the ability to relate, and the ability to create order.

Ability to Choose

The way your family brought you up is the way you tend to see the world. You don't necessarily think the same or see eye-to-eye with them; if anything, generations are often differentiated by what they value in life. But it's not so much your parents' preferences that shape your life but the way they have handled life itself, thus modeling emotional responses. In these relationships, you are gathering tools with which to respond to life—tools that may or may not work. But they are tools, nonetheless, that you learned when you were a child.

A Backpack of Tools

I like to think of childhood as a time when we collect tools in a backpack that we learn to use to handle life. Once that backpack is full, you don't learn many new emotional skills. And since your backpack is full, you naturally reach in and pull out the most appropriate tool to respond to any situation. You may even have a preset order of how you use the tools, starting with, say, one emotion, moving to a thought, and then saying a phrase you have always said.

Perhaps when you are stuck in traffic. you turn into a raging animal. You start feeling frustrated, and your hands tighten around the wheel. Then you picture the other driver as an inept or selfish person, even though you can't see or know them. Finally, you blurt out the word "Idiot!"

I'm not talking about a response to a truly dangerous driver who nearly killed your family with erratic, even drunken, driving. I'm talking about your all-too-common response of anger almost every time you get in the car. That's when you're reaching into your emotional backpack and applying a response (a tool) in an attempt to deal with the situation at hand.

If your parents and family equipped you to use the correct tools in life, you would properly use one of those tools in the appropriate situation. The problem arises when you don't have the correct tool, so you use another in its stead. It's a bit like being handed a screwdriver to help you work on your car. Many jobs that involve the need of a screwdriver will work well for you, but when it comes to changing the tire or cleaning the filters, a screwdriver offers no help. You may even successfully find ways to fix things the screwdriver wasn't meant for, but eventually, both the screwdriver and the thing you're working on will break more quickly.

What compounds the problem of using the screwdriver in life is that when we lack the right tools, we tend to overcompensate. For some people, overcompensation works to their advantage—like my friend Craig. Because he had dyslexia when he was young, he had to work harder at studying, and it trained him to put more effort into everything he did in life. The result was speedier promotions at work simply because he had such an intense work ethic. But when you apply overcompensation to areas that stretch you too thin, your relationships are ready to break.

For example, if you grew up poor, you may be so concerned that your kids should never experience your childhood poverty that you shower them with too many gifts and material possessions. You are trying to calm the childhood emotion of inner pain more than you are protecting your kids from it. If anything, you now set them up for the inverse problem of being spoiled by preventing them from knowing how to work for something and be content with what they have. They grow up with the emotion of getting what they want, and when it doesn't happen in their adulthood, they freak out. Further, you maintain and increase financial constraints because you're spending money to satisfy an emotional need that should be earmarked for other needs such as becoming debt-free, savings, retirement, education, the mission field, you name it.

Your screwdriver may be what my father-in-law calls "honey," "funny," or "money," the three basic tools for numbing painful emotions. "Honey" is the physical, like sex; "funny" is crazy thinking; and "money" is power, like control.

Many people use food as their screwdriver to fix emotions. Others use sex, TV, toys, overworking, exercise—all good things when used in the right way. How many times have you seen an older man who leaves his wife of thirty years only to marry a girl who is younger than one of his daughters? It happens. And it's disproportionate. It doesn't make sense, and it doesn't create appropriate good. John Eldredge says a man like this is trying to fill in gaps in his past. The man feels like he missed out on some young love and is trying to relive it, fill in the gap, and calm the negative emotion.

Maybe you are in certain situations in your life because you don't know how to choose properly, or even worse, you won't accept that you don't know how to choose. Have you learned the skill of waiting and being patient? An old adage goes like this: "The only thing worse than waiting is wishing you had waited."

Ability to Relate

The law dictates that a child cannot be married to an adult or another child. Only an adult can be married to another adult. It's illegal for an adult to marry a child because a child does not have the mental or emotional capacity to act and make choices as a spouse. Yet every day, people who remain emotionally stuck in their childhood get married and expect to have a functional adult emotional relationship with a spouse.

It can't work. It doesn't work. Just as the law only recognizes two consenting *adults* being married to each other, so does the Blueprint. You can't obtain the right results in an illegal manner.

Being raised by parents who were still children emotionally usually swings your emotions in one of two ways. Either you act like a child in the same way they did, or you take on an overdeveloped sense of responsibility at an early age.

Philip came to me because his relationship with his girlfriend had broken down. He had emotionally shut down and couldn't summon the energy to be in the relationship with the girl he thought he wanted to marry. We chatted about whether there were any red flags in their relationship that would warrant his desire to not be with her anymore. From his description of her, it didn't appear the problem lay with her.

"Tell me about your childhood and your mum and dad's relationship."

"I grew up not far from here. We were pretty poor and struggled to make ends meet. That was probably because my dad left when I was ten and didn't support us with money or anything else. My mom had to raise us four children by herself, and I just remember never having enough."

"Tell me more of what it was like at home when your dad left."

"It was tough. My mom was angry and never talked about anything with us. My sisters just did their own thing, and I felt I had to look after them and my little brother. We all just survived really."

"When things got really tough or there was an argument to settle in the house, who would step in to referee it, or make decisions or take on responsibilities?"

"Well, I did. I was the oldest boy. I mean, my mom did her best, but she was at work most of the time, and I would make sure things were cleaned up and that my siblings did their homework and got something to eat. I just became the man of the house, I guess."

"Did you feel if you didn't do these things, your family would fall apart?"

"Of course. My dad wasn't around, and my brother and sisters needed me."

What Philip had done was assume an adult role at a very early age to care for siblings at a level that shouldn't have been his responsibility. It created an overdeveloped sense of responsibility in him to be responsible for others and now the romantic relationship with his girl-friend was draining him because he only felt the burden to make it work and couldn't enjoy it. It brought past emotions to the surface of when he last had to be responsible for others. He felt like he was raising his siblings all over again, and the emotions of that ten-year-old boy were painful.

Children can assume coping mechanisms in a family that they use to survive. This is especially true in situations when the parent is abusive. Abused children learn to predict their parent's behavior so they can respond to the signs indicating the parent may get angry and abusive. They become watchers of that behavior, constantly assessing in order to immediately change their response to the situation of the moment, then placate their parent and minimize the potential of danger to themselves.

I've seen this manifest itself in marriages time and again where one spouse will do whatever the other spouse wants just so they don't have to deal with confrontation. They learned this by watching and responding in their childhood, taking on adult responsibilities when they should have had the freedom to be a child. I have heard people say they had to "grow up fast." But that often indicates they didn't grow up and learn how to relate properly.

This, of course, isn't exclusive to those who have learned this behavior in their childhood. Adults can be forced into this submissive role without having seen it as a child. But I've seen it more commonly in people who learned that dysfunctional submissive role early on. A lack of appropriate parenting affects your ability to have healthy relationships with your friends, spouse, and children. Being a spouse and being a parent demand a lot of you every day. A child can't do it, and your child-emotions can't do it either.

Ability to Create Order

The book *Doing the Best I Can*,[1] coauthored by Kathryn Edin and Timothy J. Nelson, investigates the topic of fatherhood in the inner city. In an interview, Professor Edin said she had assumed that young men who became fathers were only after the sex and had no interest in fatherhood.[2] She considered them careless, deadbeat dads who weren't expecting to have a child and didn't want to be around when one came along.

But her research revealed something different. Most of the young men were around at their child's birth, and most of them made a concerted effort to create a family unit by moving in with the child's mother. One year later, however, well over fifty percent of these young fathers had left the relationship, the home, and were not fully participating in their child's life if at all.

Professor Edin noticed an interesting phrase and comment that most of the young men made when they initially ventured into their attempt at carrying out the role of a father. They said, "I wanna be there for my kid." Pressed further on what that meant, they overwhelmingly responded with comments like "I wanna be there for my kid because my father wasn't there for me."

They had identified the pain they felt growing up without their father present in their lives. The problem was that even with the intentions of being there, they ultimately couldn't make it work the way they had wanted, dreamed, or planned to. Why? Because their dads didn't give them the tools to be a husband or a father.

What these young fathers were missing was the ability to create order. It's amazing that most people have an idea of the Blueprint of normal relationships impressed in their desires, but they can't make it happen. Making it happen is not just a matter of intention but of ability, and those abilities are what create order in your life, your marriage, and your children's lives.

Changing These Three Affected Abilities

In the next chapter, we will look at the three steps required to change the effects of the first four relationships and replace the tools you have in your backpack.

But first, a couple of things to consider: God made it a point to say in Genesis 2 that a man should *leave* his parents and be joined to his wife (and women are to leave their parents too). What I am presenting is not about leaving home or being independent; it's about cutting off inherited learned behaviors, habits, and baggage from your past relationships that will affect your ability to become one with your spouse and set up a great Blueprint for your kids. Many believe if they can just leave home and have control over their own life, somehow everything will be fine. But years later, they discover that they still don't have the tools they need to make their marriage work, be a good employee, or be a present parent.

The other issue is that some will say you can't blame anyone else—that everyone needs to take responsibility for themselves. I would agree but only so far. It's true: We make our own choices; we own our own sin; we create our own chaos or order. But even God acknowledged that every choice has a beginning point. And that beginning is often found in your parents' actions, words, and choices that you observed as a child. In Genesis 3:9-11, God was walking in the cool of day to look for Adam and Eve and He found them hiding in a bush.

"Why are you hiding?" He said.

"Because we were naked," they said.

"Who said you were naked?" God asked.

Do you see what happened there? God connected the dots that Adam and Eve's present words, actions, and thinking were tied to someone or something else. God knew He hadn't designed that shame into them. His Blueprint didn't have any place for it. So it must have come from something outside the Blueprint.

What compelled Adam and Eve to act against the way they were designed? Why do we say and do the things that we don't really want? Why do we fail at disciplining ourselves to change our behavior and feelings?

In the next chapter, we will explore the hidden reasons that drive our actions and beliefs. We will discover the subconscious choices we make every day that secretly control us. And finally, we will learn how to deal with those choices in a positive way.

CHAPTER 6

Three-Step Roadmap: Step One, Deal with the Root

It's about the root, not the fruit.

When I was nine years old, my parents bought an old house that needed a lot of work. It had a sizable garden that had not been tended properly in a very long time. After a while, we launched into it as a family and hacked away lots of bushes. The garden looked beautiful, but eventually, the inevitable happened: All the bushes grew back.

My mother knew that all the stumps and roots had to be dug up, and I didn't escape her recruitment. Have you ever dug up deep roots with a shovel? It seems to take forever, and just one root hidden at the bottom of the stump can halt the task. What's worse is that you can't see any of the roots until you have dug and dug and dug.

When the job is finally done, you roll the stump aside with great relief, only to be underwhelmed by its size. How did such a small root put up such a great fight?

So many people become discouraged because they apply discipline and faith to their issues, only to find themselves repeating behaviors and experiences with the same emotions. I suggest it's because discipline is like hacking the branches or even picking the bad fruit off a tree, only to have it grow back again. Instead, we need to cut the bad root off the tree—in this case, our family tree.

Examining your past relationships can seem much like our family's experiment in the garden. And let me tell you, once you cut the bad root, the bad fruit *never* comes back.

The following diagram is my suggestion of how our family tree works:

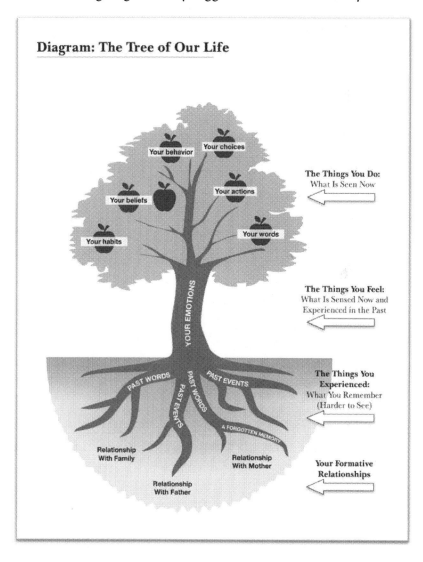

Diagram: The Tree of Our Life

The Things You Do:
What Is Seen Now

The Things You Feel:
What Is Sensed Now and Experienced in the Past

The Things You Experienced:
What You Remember (Harder to See)

Your Formative Relationships

A Description of the Tree of Your Life

The preceding diagram shows how the flow of experience and emotions operates in our lives as follows:

The Fruit: Nothing you do—your choices, actions, habits, and even your beliefs and words—is created in a vacuum. These things are the fruit of everything else you have experienced. They are your responses to life, partially created by you and partially instilled in you from your childhood. They are your responsibility to deal with and to choose to create good fruit. However, because of your past emotions manifesting in your present, you are often powerless to choose better. These emotions control and dictate your choices.

Discipline alone cannot change the fruit. It can remove it for a time, but because the fruit is a product of the tree's nature, it will keep coming back. An orange tree produces oranges. An apple tree produces apples. Only a change of nature can change the fruit.

The Trunk (Your Emotions): This forms the body of the tree. Everything that has happened to you created a feeling, an emotion. God has made us more than carbon and chemicals; we are spirit and truth. The spirit is tied to our emotions, and the truth is the facts of our life. The trunk is the core, the driving power of our lives.

God's original Blueprint design laid out that these emotions should result in the fruits of the spirit: love, joy, peace, patience, kindness, and so on. When your emotions are out of proportion to an event you are experiencing, you know something hidden below the surface has dictated this response. Experiencing the emotions of a child as an adult reveals that you have not matured beyond a past event. Your emotions are frozen in time and tied to the past event that can be brought up again and experienced through current events.

The Roots (Past Events and Words): Everything you are has been formed by past events and words spoken (or even unspoken) to you. God created everything by His words, and we are created by words spoken and unspoken within our first four relationships. These words and events form the pattern of how the rest of the tree will grow. They are things you had no control over as a child. They were chosen for you.

As children, we depend on our parents and family to teach us, show us, and speak to us all the things we will need to become functional and mature adults. For the words and events you chose as a child, your parents had the responsibility to navigate you back, to discipline you, to teach you the right way.

Wherever these events and words did not follow the pattern of the Blueprint God gave us, we are hindered in our emotions and responses in life. Unfortunately, because these events are in the past, they are like roots buried in the ground, not easily seen or understood. This is why trying to figure out what specific experiences in your past caused an emotion to dictate how you feel and respond today can be difficult. We must ask ourselves where an emotion that manifests today began and took root.

The Formative Relationships: These are the first four relationships we had, discussed in earlier chapters. We are entirely dependent on them to create the events, experiences, and words we need to teach us how to be the mature, functional adults God's Blueprint designed us to be.

Our Roadmap: Root, Return, Replace

Here are the three steps we will now consider in our roadmap to being free from bad roots that control our lives. They are three steps that will truly help you to do what seems impossible: change the nature of the tree, allowing it to produce good fruit. The first step: Deal with the root of bitterness and forgiveness. The second: Return burdens and assign responsibility. The third: Replace the tools and move on.

In the remainder of this chapter, we will look at only the first step.

A Bitter Root

For many years, Johnny Barr was my father's best friend. He lived in one of the rougher parts of London, pastoring an Elim Pentecostal church for many years. He had become pretty well-known in Christian circles but, like my dad, shunned stardom. What made him so sought after was his incredible ability to pinpoint a person's problem. He called it "prophetic counselling"; we called it "amazing."

"The Church of England would send me their most difficult counselling cases," he once said to me. "But they probably won't admit to that," he would chuckle.

I could believe it. I worked under him a few times and saw how many clamored to seek his counsel, and he graciously saw everyone he could. Of the many things I learned from Johnny, he said one particular thing time and again: "You must always deal with a root of bitterness in a person."

Bitterness! I don't know how many times I heard him say bitterness was the cause of problems, and I got to the point where, when he said it again, I said to myself, *Come on, Johnny! It can't always be a root of bitterness.* Yet in the twenty short years I have been mentoring and counselling, I have realized he was right.

Bitterness occurs when rejection and pride combine to make a deep anger within you. There is only one way to rid yourself of any of it, and that's simple forgiveness. Forgiveness heals rejection and breaks pride. And when rejection and pride have gone, the fire of anger has no fuel.

Bitterness is always a signal that you have been rejected in some way. If you weren't given attention, if you were abused in some way, if you were abandoned, if you were treated unfairly, if you were forced to grow up instead of be a child in childhood, if someone withheld affection from you, if you were burdened with stress when you shouldn't have been, if your parents allowed you to worry about their financial problems, if you weren't taught things you think you should have been, if your dad gave more time to his job, friends, or life—whatever it is, it always ends up in some level of bitterness.

Fairy tales tend to portray bitterness as an old hag gnarled with anger and revenge for some form of injustice. That may not be what you look like on the outside, but it's there on the inside. Eventually, that gnarled, bitter side will manifest in your relationships and body—if not on your face.

The bad fruit that comes from bitterness literally kills you. Proverbs 14:30 says it rots the bones. The marrow of your bones is where the white blood cells, which heal your body, are produced. In other words, your body ends up killing itself because of bitterness.

Science proves this. The documentary *Stress: Portrait of a Killer* by National Geographic[1] proves that stress literally blocks up your arteries, retards brain cell growth, and causes your DNA to degrade. Your body can't sustain itself and eventually dies.

The book *How Children Learn* by Paul Tough[2] discusses how people who don't succeed in life usually had stressful childhoods. The author is an economist who, in his investigation on how to improve the economics of schools in the U.S., discovered a huge underlying problem that could not be fixed with economic know-how. He followed up with people to learn how they had fared in life after their failure or success at school. He discovered that a person's current frustration and anger (bitterness) is connected to their inability to control their present life, evidenced by their increased difficulties in getting a good job, being able to maintain a relationship, or not feeling stupid. He then determined that their current problems could be traced back to their childhood.

It works like this: If a child has to endure a stressful environment and doesn't know how to handle it or doesn't have someone to handle it for them, they then take on the responsibility to process it in their mind and emotions through a fight-or-flight response. This response induces increased adrenaline and cortisol that make them, among other things, very reactive. When such children are placed in the classroom, their brains can't properly develop because the stress stops neurons from connecting properly.

Imagine being a child and wondering whether you'll be evicted this week, if you will eat tomorrow, or if your father will beat you up when you get home. Then someone asks you to answer a math question. You can't; your brain can't process it all at once. The problem then compounds because you fall behind educationally, feel stupid, and act out emotionally in a myriad of ways. The stress retards your learning ability as your parents deny you the tools to handle life properly.

Please note: Stress is not all bad. To exercise your body and condition it to be stronger, you must put your body under stress. Stressing and slightly tearing the muscles causes them to grow bigger and stronger. But this is not a constant, uncontrolled stress; it is a productive stress—different from the type that kills us. In order to avoid killer stress, we must discover the tools that make us mature and stronger and help us overcome and handle life, no matter what it throws our way.

At this point, it would be easy to assume I believe we are in our current condition through no fault of our own. Let me make it clear: It may be someone else's fault that you are where you are because of your childhood. But it is most assuredly your problem now, and it is most assuredly your responsibility to choose to stay the way you are or do something about it. God has given us the Blueprint and steps to change ourselves to match it. And the first step is forgiveness.

Forgiveness First

Forgiveness must come first in this process because nothing else works without it. It's not easy, because it's a choice and not a feeling, and invariably the choice will move you to the opposite of what you feel. Forgiveness seems so powerless; it seems to let the perpetrator off scot-free and fail to fix any present frustration. But there is one very logical reason to forgive: You can't move on from the past if you still live there. You're not going to stop thinking about a person if you keep wanting to kill them or force them to pay the price you believe they should pay.

To be clear, these are not always conscious thoughts but are often patterns of thinking born out of a belief, accurate or not, that an injustice has been done to you. Your thought patterns react and keep you in a state of demanding justice. That demanded justice is often acted out through current situations that have nothing to do with the original unjust act. If you haven't consciously and actively forgiven that original act of injustice, you are not disconnected from it.

Please know, forgiveness is not about changing the past but about changing your future. It's not about saying the wrong thing done to you is now OK; it is most definitely about removing its power, making it dead to you. A painful event from the past can powerfully exist in your present emotions and feed your bitterness. You must be resolved to be done with it, and the only way is forgiveness.

Make no mistake; you can't just choose to be above this past event, forget about it, or discipline yourself out of thinking about it. A change of thinking or behavior alone will not disconnect you from bitterness. Forgiveness is for your heart. Remember, you are trying to cut a root that connects your present self to a past event. They can both exist, but they do not have to be connected anymore. Forgiveness is the only way to disconnect the two.

I love words. The dictionary gives us the most common meanings for the word *forgive*, but when I read the Bible, I love discovering a word's literal meaning. The literal Greek translation of Jesus's use of the word *forgive* is "An intense sending forth of 'letting-go' or leaving." [3] Even the translation acknowledges that this word is intense and requires some level of force to carry out. It also indicates a separation is happening, in other words, the cutting off of a root.

Allow me to connect some dots. If you are a Christ-follower, you will know that Jesus said if you forgive others, then and only then can you get forgiveness from God for yourself, and vice versa if you don't forgive (see Matt. 6). Our entire life is a journey back to our relationship with God, ultimately restoring his original plan to be with Him and live out the life He has designed for us.

In this Blueprint, His plan, the first relationship you ever had was with God. And in this very clear and concise directive, Jesus gives us the first step to getting back to the Blueprint and fixing our broken relationships. It is of utmost importance that this happen first. I have found that when a person does not choose to forgive, no other following step will make a difference in their life. If you do not accept and act on this revelation, you may as well put this book down now.

Some people to whom I have shown this step have responded, "I need to go away and pray about that."

"When you come back, I will have nothing else for you until you've chosen forgiveness," I tell them. No new information will work until they have disconnected themselves from bitter thoughts and emotions. And at this point, it's a choice.

CHAPTER 7

Three-Step Roadmap: Step Two, Return the Burden

Brad came to my office many years ago because he was at his wit's end. Now in his mid-fifties, he loved Harley Davidsons and had a "man's man" demeanor. Brad had no intention of coming to speak to a pastor, but his brother convinced him to meet with me.

"I'm a mess," he admitted when I pressed him. "My fifth wife just left me. And we've only been married a year."

"Why do you think she left?"

"Oh, I know why." He went on to tell me about an addiction to porn that he just couldn't shake.

"Why did your other wives leave you?"

"Same reason."

In my years of counseling other men who have dealt with porn addiction, the underlying issue always seems to be a need for power and/or comfort. I asked Brad to tell me about his mum, and he started to cry. "She died of cancer when I was eight years old," he said through his tears. After he told me more about his childhood after losing his mother, I knew what to say.

"Your addiction to porn isn't about the naked women or even about your wives not satisfying you physically," I said. "You still want your mum to hold you. You want to bury your head in her chest and feel safe again, because only she could have given you that when you were saddest," I said.

He let out a deep sob.

Most people who have a burden in their lives today picked it up in their past and froze emotionally at that moment. Emotionally, Brad was still stuck at eight years old and couldn't move on. Neither his father or anyone else had helped him deal with the trauma of losing his mother. His relationships kept dying because he couldn't give others what they needed, and they couldn't give him what he needed. Somehow, he had to return emotionally to his eight-year-old setpoint, let go of his burden, and move forward.

Identify, Assign, Return

This second step, returning the burden, has three parts: identify the burden, assign it, and return it to whom it belongs. People often carry burdens they can't identify, many of them belonging to someone else. Moreover, they often expect the wrong people to resolve the burden they're carrying.

I find it amazing, for example, that we translate emotions of our past through events in our present. You may get upset about an issue with, say, your wife, and think your frustration is only about the way she does something. But sometimes your frustration has arisen out of a present emotion tied to a past event. The easiest way to identify whether this is true is to examine how proportionate your frustration is to the infraction you are reacting to. When the size of your emotion of anger, fear, hurt, or rejection outweighs the size of the infraction, it is acceptable to assume that your emotion is also connected to something else, usually a past event.

Identify the Burden

A husband I once mentored became blazing mad at his wife because she didn't clean up the house. I told him to either clean the house himself or find someone else to do it. Problem solved. But he still felt disrespected by his wife. So once I led the conversation to its logical end, he had to admit either she was making a concerted effort to irritate him or his anger was disproportionate to the perceived crime and therefore, not about her housekeeping at all.

After more discussion, I discovered that while he was growing up, his mother had abandoned him. His wife's actions brought up the same emotion—feeling uncared for—as his mother's abandonment.

This man had taken an emotion from the past and brought it forward. He thought his anger only related to the untidy house. But he was assigning responsibility for his emotional burden to the wrong person. I helped him identify his unresolved feelings of being uncared for by his mother.

I highly recommend a counselor or mentor who can help you identify your real burden. Having the aid of someone else is the best step in this process; they can ask logical questions and help you compare your experience to that found in the Blueprint. Since our emotions tend to blind us, if you are angry or hurt, you will always have a way to justify what you feel or believe. A counselor or mentor can help you discern between your self-protecting logic and the Blueprint that reveals an area you need to deal with.

Questions to Ask Yourself to Help Identify the Burden
- When was the first time I felt this emotion/burden?
- What happened? Who was there?

- What should have happened?
- If nothing could have changed the event, what should my parents have done to help me handle the situation? What should I have done?

Assign the Burden

Belinda had been a busy, successful executive at a well-known corporation. After she was downsized in the economic downturn, each of her subsequent jobs seemed to shrink in pay. An empty-nester and divorcee, she was squeezing every penny she could earn. She didn't ask for help or broadcast her trials, but she was more and more frustrated with her situation. Yes, life was difficult, but her disproportionate emotional turmoil didn't match her suck-it-up-and-get-on-with-it ethos.

"This doesn't make sense," I told her. "Why are you so upset? You list all the blessings you have. But then you chasten yourself for being mad about not having what you say you don't necessarily deserve?

"You're saying you should be happy, yet you're not. Your anger is not about your financial situation. So what's it really about?"

Again, I always follow the Blueprint and ask about the first four relationships a person should have. Then, I look for the time the person first felt the same emotions they are now feeling.

"Belinda, you talk like you're mad at God for not helping you out. Your speech sounds like something I'd expect to hear from a child who's mad at Daddy. So tell me about your dad."

As it turned out, her dad had left the family when Belinda was a young girl, a day she vividly remembers.

"What did he say when he left?" I asked.

"He said he had to go because he and my mom were not getting along. He said she had asked him to leave, and he couldn't do anything about it—that it was her fault he was leaving, not his."

"What did you say to him?"

She paused. "Nothing! What could I say? I was seven years old."

"Let me get this straight. Your dad is leaving. He is blaming your mum for leaving and you, his daughter, said nothing. Is that right?"

"Yes."

"Doesn't it make sense that a seven-year-should want to shout 'Daddy, don't leave! I don't want you to leave!' Isn't it the right of that child to have her father stay and be her father? It's his job to tell his wife, 'You may not want me around anymore, but I'm going to fight to be around my kids and be a father to them.' He should have fought tooth and nail to be in your life, but he willingly left because he was asked to. That's not a father!

"Aren't those the things you wish you had said?" I added. "Belinda, it seems to me you have to let that seven-year-old girl who is still inside you have her say. She didn't get to say anything, and she needs to let it out. She needs to tell her dad that the burden she's been carrying doesn't belong to her. It belongs to him. He created it."

She agreed.

Assigning the burden happens when you place the responsibility for what caused the burden at the feet of the person who brought it about. Most often, a person who has carried a burden since childhood has done so, like Belinda, because their parent(s) failed to properly carry out their responsibilities.

If you don't identify who was at fault for creating the burden you still carry, you will continue to carry it. Forgiveness must go to a person, a perpetrator, who created the burden. You may have been the one who created it, but all the same, we are never bitter toward an event. We feel bitter, angry, hurt, or rejected by a person.

Questions to Help you Assign the Burden:

- Who created the situation that made me feel so rejected and angry?

- Who could have stopped it or avoided it from happening?

*If more than one person is responsible, which one carries the ultimate responsibility?

Return the Burden

"Belinda," I said. "I want you to do several things. First, I want you to write a letter to your dad. You don't have to send it unless you want to; you just have to write it."

Somehow, she had to let that seven-year-old inside her say the words she had held in for 40 years.

"I want you to tell your dad first that you've realized the struggles you have in your present life are connected to your past, specifically, your relationship with him. Then admit you were angry with him and ask forgiveness for the bitterness you held against him all these years."

Next, I asked her to say the most difficult words of all. "Dad, you left me when I was seven years old. You blamed Mom for your departure, but you had no right to leave. You should have fought to be around for me. It wasn't my job to grow up without a father; it was your job to make sure I had one: you!

"This burden I have carried was one you created, and I'm giving it back to you now. Please know, I forgive you for abandoning me, I love you, and I want to have a proper healthy relationship with you without this deep resentment inside. I'm done carrying that burden. Today."

Those were going to be hard words to say. All her fears came to the surface: *What will he say? What is he going to think? He'll hate me. This will just open up old wounds. This may devastate him.*

These were all real fears, but they were not Belinda's problem. That may sound harsh, but it is not the job of a seven-year-old to carry the burden that belongs to the parent. The Blueprint must be put back into order. Speaking up may devastate the parent, but it's their job to resolve it; it's their job to heal it; it's their job to deal with it—and they can.

Only the parent can carry their own burden. The child can't do that for the parent. Belinda couldn't make her father be a father, yet she longed for one. The good news is that everyone *can* have a father, even in adulthood, which we'll talk about later. But know this: You can't properly create a fatherly relationship with God or someone else in your life until you have reassigned the burden of fatherlessness to the one who created it: your father.

This may sound odd, but the "present you" must help the "past you" get those words out and reassign the burden. The forty-year-old you must give the voice to the emotions of the seven-year-old you and help that child grow up emotionally. I've seen people do this many times, and you'd be amazed at how unburdened they become when they've finished the process.

I realize some may think it cruel to take time years later to tell a man who abandoned his child that he was a horrible father. "Doesn't he already know this? Isn't it digging up the past? He's had to live with this guilt for years!"

All this may be true, but it doesn't supersede the order set forth in the Blueprint: The father, not the child, has the responsibility to carry the burden. I have seen so many relationships repaired because someone took the time and trouble to bring up the problem. Family members can now speak words of healing to each other when they couldn't—or didn't think they had the right to—say them before. The father may himself have been abandoned by his father and didn't know how to parent. If this is the case, he, too, should follow the Blueprint and put things into order. You would be setting an example he could follow.

Feeling sorry for your father or other family member doesn't fix the situation. What's more, we must do this for the sake of our children as an example to them. They are dependent on us teaching them the way of the Blueprint.

Allow me to say that sending a letter is not a requirement. To do so or not is your choice, best taken under advisement from your mentor. You may write the letter and not send it. You may use someone else as a proxy to act as the person to whom you need to say these words. You could read the letter to that proxy or to a mentor.

This step is not about talking to that original person or blaming them. Instead, it's about removing the burden from yourself and putting it back into order where it lies. I believe the order demands that you bookend the conversation with forgiveness: you subjecting your own bitterness to repentance and extending forgiveness to the one who hurt you. It's about reassigning the proper order of responsibility.

Unfortunately for Belinda, her father *did* go ballistic when he received the letter that she eventually chose to send. After reading it, he called her up and told her she was ungrateful and that he had done everything he could, that if she had been a better daughter, she would be further on in life.

This did not surprise me. Belinda's father's voice is one of bitterness and anger, the voice of the child within him reacting and using the broken tools he has to fix his present situation.

"Did his reaction make your relationship better or worse?" I asked her.

"Neither," she said.

This is exactly right, because Belinda never had a proper relationship with her father in the first place. He couldn't make her feel any worse than he already had; he had abandoned her. All her fears of being rejected once again didn't materialize, even though he was rejecting her again. Why? Because she was now listening to him as a forty-something-year-old woman whose seven-year-old emotions had now grown up. She was now in the position of listening to him rant like a child and being able to speak with peace about how she could help him move forward, too. She could see she didn't have a negative reaction to him anymore. She had handed him back the burden and had forgiven him. What's more, years later, Belinda told me she and her father had grown closer because she was no longer reacting to him as a wounded child.

Let me say again that it is not heartless to lay this burden at the other person's feet. If it belongs to them, give it to them. This is not about accusation or being angry or bitter; you should have already dealt with that through forgiveness. If you fail to go through forgiveness first, you are not reassigning the burden, you are accusing.

But as I said earlier, a child cannot carry the responsibility that only an adult should carry. You must first help yourself to grow up emotionally. Then you can go back to the person who hurt you and help them grow up if, first, they want to do so, and second, you have the ability to help them.

Remember, people are responsible to change themselves once they become adults. God has not left us abandoned and without help. He offers Himself as our healer, our hope, and our Father.

At this point, if you have followed the process and become unburdened, you will see with new eyes. And several things should have happened:

- You should feel grown up. You no longer feel the tormented childhood emotions within you because you're done with the bitterness.

- You should feel more alive. The story of the prodigal son in Luke 15 portrays the son at a turning point where he realizes he has rejected his father, messed up his life, and must go back to restore his relationship. When he realizes what he must do, Scripture says he "came to his senses" (Luke 15:17a). This is such a telling phrase, because it involves more than just realizing you were wrong. It includes suddenly being connected to your senses at full capacity.

Science proves that depression stops you from feeling joy in the things you experience. Freedom literally makes everything seem greater: food tastes better, music sounds sweeter, conversations are exhilarating, opportunities are exciting, challenges are thrilling, and life in general becomes more wonderful.

- You should have a new compassion for the one who burdened you. My father-in-law often uses a particular phrase: "Usually, people are more to be pitied than scorned." This means that once you become free, you start to see the brokenness within your own parent/family, and you also see the wonderful things they did. They may not have given you certain tools in life because they didn't receive those tools themselves.

This is having the eyes of God: Accepting people for who they are without tripping up over who they are not, and then responsibly making efforts to restore them as well. Chances are good that your family did give you great things, but you haven't been able to access them, because unforgiveness disconnects us from the power of those good things.

Another person who followed this returning process and wrote a letter to his mother was Glen.

Glen came to me in a bad place relationally. His marriage was breaking up. He didn't trust his wife, yet the two were very codependent. He was a jovial person by nature and could brighten any room he walked into, but there was only one person he couldn't make happy: his wife.

After much discussion, I could see he was in a difficult place. In fact, his wife had recently moved out and decided to live with someone else. He didn't know what to do and was stuck . He felt like a failure.

But what didn't make sense to me was how responsible he felt for his wife leaving him. "Did you do something to make her leave?" I asked, wondering if he had neglected her in some way or even abused her. As far as I could tell, he had been a gold-star husband when it came to giving her attention and providing for her needs and desires. And I had no reason to believe this wasn't true. Something didn't make sense.

My question for him at this point wasn't so much about why she had left him or what he had done to make her leave him. It was why he felt such an overdeveloped sense of responsibility for her actions. Glen had only blamed himself for her departure. It seemed, from his perspective, his wife bore no responsibility.

Again, I followed the Blueprint and discovered that his mother had left his father, his sister and him when he was a boy. I wanted to find out whether he had processed all the emotions of that past event.

"Glen, have you ever talked to your mum about her leaving you when you were a boy?"

"No."

"Why not?"

"I don't really know. It was so long ago that it doesn't seem important anymore."

I could tell by the way Glen was refusing to hold his wife responsible for her part in leaving him that there was a good chance he had never held his mother responsible for her part in leaving him as a boy. Yet he obviously still felt rejected by both of their actions.

Once I explained to him the importance of returning the burden back to the source and allowing himself to stop bearing it, I asked him to write a letter to his mum with no obligation to send it to her. Again, it was to allow the older version of himself to empower the younger version to say the words he never got a chance to say.

A week later, I received a call from Glen.

"Well, I did it," he said.

"Oh, good. You wrote the letter."

"No, I spoke to my mom. I wrote the letter; then I called her up and asked if I could read it to her."

Wow! Glen had gone a step further than I expected. It turns out that when he had called her about the letter, he burst into tears so intense that his mum, concerned, wanted to meet him immediately. They did so that day in a car at a gas station. He told her it would be best if he could read the letter he had written to her.

"So how did it go?" I asked.

"It was amazing. After I read my letter to her, she was in tears. And she apologized for everything she did. She told me where she was emotionally when she left. And we talked. We just talked. It was so great."

I could see a weight had lifted off his shoulders.

Glen was now ready to tackle the issues in his marriage because he was no longer approaching it like an abandoned child trying to protect his mother from feeling bad. I can only imagine how good the gift of forgiveness felt to his mother and how great the freedom he enjoyed in his heart.

Template for the Letter

I imagine you haven't written many letters like the one I'm suggesting. So let me give you a suggested template of what you should write:

> Dear (person's name),
>
> I am writing to you about something that has bothered me for a while now. I want to start by saying how much I love you and …. *(insert your words of love, admiration, or thanks if appropriate; and if you have none, just leave this sentence out)*.
>
> Recently, I have realized I've been holding something against you, and I have been angry. I want to apologize for my bitterness against you, because nothing good ever comes from that. I was wrong.
>
> When I was *(age)* I remember . . . *(explain the situation of the thing that happened that the person did or didn't do that hurt you, and/or explain the words they said. Don't offer reasons for why they did it or to explain away or diminish what they did.*

Neither should you over-speak the description of the event, lest you become accusatory. Just say plainly what happened.) It was your fault. You were responsible for *(list their responsibility as an adult).*

I now realize I must stop holding onto this. I need to move on in my life and stop blaming you for it. So, I want you to know I forgive you. I forgive you for. . . *(List any things you think you need to be clear about of what you forgive).*

Please know I love you and want to have a better relationship with you. *(Note: only write this last line if it is appropriate to write; take the advice of your counselor/mentor in this).*

Thank you for taking the time to read this.

(Your signature)

At this point, I should say that if the infraction perpetrated against you was illegal, you should take advice on whether to pursue legal action. This is especially true if you were a child when it happened and the wrong was of the sexual nature. Sexual crimes are heinous, and in recent years, there has been an increase in people pursuing legal justice against those who committed a sexual crime against them in childhood or in adulthood. I especially support legal action to both limit further abuse the perpetrator could inflict on others and to change any culture that would support the abuse by doing nothing.

However, this does not mean you are a bad person if you don't report a wrong. Digging up past traumas by writing a letter can be hard enough for many people without adding further self-harm by adding a legal process too. Please, talk to a counselor about this if it applies to you.

One more thing. In this process, you may recognize that you are the one who has been the perpetrator to someone else. You are the one who should receive a letter written by someone else. You are one of the first four relationships to someone else, and you created a burden they carried.

We don't have room to address such problems entirely in this book, but I want to encourage you that if it's true of you, you should consider giving the other person the best gift you can give by apologizing for what you did or said. You may be able to write a letter and admit to what you did, say you are sorry, that they have a right to be angry at you, but you are asking for their forgiveness. If they are an adult now, you have no power to dictate what they should feel about you or how they should respond in life. That season has passed. But you can offer something good that could help them move closer to resolving that past hurt you caused.

You can at least remove the self-doubt they may have had as a child, wondering what they did wrong to make you reject and hurt them. Of course, to do that, you would have to say or write your remorse for them to consider. Just writing the letter and not sending it will not help them at all.

If this paragraph has struck a nerve with you, you should circle back to consider following my suggestions. I acknowledge the fact that if what you did was criminal, writing such a letter could place you in a legally precarious position. Get an attorney's advice on this before writing any letter.

And finally, pray. James 1:5 tells us, "If any of you lacks wisdom, you should ask God, who gives generously to all without finding fault, and it will be given to you."

CHAPTER 8

Three-Step Roadmap:
Step Three, Replace the Tool

Reordering the responsibility

D an was a great guy, the type of person you could depend on to be a trusted friend. He wasn't outwardly swayed by events, good or bad, but rather was an even-keeled, quiet soul. He seemed reserved but not aloof, unmoved but not uncaring.

Dan and I met to chat about something that was bothering him. Usually what troubles a person internally will show up in events or relationships around them, and they will want to talk about that event or relationship. In Dan's case, his concerns were showing up in his relationship with his wife.

Men will avoid talking about a marriage issue with an advisor and keep trying to find a solution by themselves; I think it's just the way they're wired. By the time they seek someone out for advice, it's only because they've finally proven they don't have the solution and are now feeling the pain of the marriage not working.

But Dan was different. He could admit that the pain he was experiencing wasn't about the marriage alone but something deeper in himself.

"Dan, what seems to be the biggest issue your marriage brings up in you?"

"I'm not sure. We have the usual problems of balancing money and schedules and cars breaking down, but it's more than that. I feel like I can't breathe sometimes. I love my wife, but I don't seem to give her the right answers. I can't make her happy."

Compounding the problem was that this was a second marriage for him, and dealing with his ex-wife and trading childcare responsibilities on the weekends was exacerbating everything. We of course talked about his upbringing to reveal that his dad was never emotionally available for him. He was a man who rarely showed emotion and never outward affection to his wife or son. Dan didn't even recall his dad showing him how to do basic things like learn how to ride a bike or change a tire. His dad, though present physically, wasn't present relationally.

"What did you see your parents do when they needed to solve a problem? How did they work out solutions together?" He shrugged his shoulders.

"Nothing," he said. "I didn't really see them interact much at all. We just lived together."

This is when I figured out there was a chance that Dan's challenge wasn't that his wife was unhappy, but that he just didn't have the tools to communicate with her. He hadn't gotten those tools from his father by direct instruction or by observation. He was treating the problems in his marriage as something he had to "fix" just to make his wife happy. And because she wasn't happy, he concluded his marriage was probably almost over.

This is where Dan began his new journey of gathering new tools to build his marriage and family in the way the Blueprint works. He had to accept the idea that his wife wasn't someone to fix. He had to learn that communication is often just listening and trusting. And he had to realize problems usually aren't as bad as he thought, especially if God is on his side and he is following in the ways God designed life to work. But most of all at this juncture in his life, he needed someone to be a source like a father and teach him how to use new tools. Everyone needs someone who can show and teach them new tools.

In your childhood and present life, you will come across real burdens and challenges; they're a part of life. We are not trying to eliminate challenges but overcome them. Even Christ commands us to take up our cross and follow Him. We must first learn the order God has designed for us, the Blueprint. Second, we must find the right tools to help us handle the challenges and burdens of life. Christ told us He did not come to take us out of the world but to help us overcome it (John 17:15). He said he had a burden for us, but that it would be easy and light. Life is not easy or comfortable, but He gives us the tools that lift those burdens (Matt. 11:30). Thank God for His wisdom and help.

Once you have reassigned the burdens and removed the wrong tools for life from your backpack, you now have space for the right tools. This is not a venture learned overnight but a relearning of habits, restoring relationships and reordering yourself to the Blueprint, especially for the benefit of your kids. These things are more caught than taught.

The problem we have today with our schools is not that they don't have lofty goals beyond educational skills to prepare children for life, but that the lessons they are now expected to teach our kids are beyond their true responsibility. They can't teach our kids how to be adults; they can't properly teach them fundamental morals; they can't give them all the life tools they will need. This is the job of the parents. Only a father and a mother (or a person who can act as father/mother in the child's life) can instill the right tools into a child. Teachers are great and needed, but they can't parent the way a parent should. They are supplemental to the position and responsibility that belongs to the parent.

So if you are without a real father or mother to give you the right tools in life, what should you do? The answer is simple: Go get what you need. Here's how it works: First, find God. Second, find a mentor. Third, get what you need.

Find God

I have counselled and mentored enough non-Christians to know that they finally have to admit there is something to this "God thing," even if they are not ready to subscribe to it. I understand they may not be at the same discovery point of God as I am, but the sense that they find in the Blueprint always blows their mind.

The problem arises, however, when they are faced with making a final decision to pursue or reject God. Why? Because aside from the deeper arguments of God's existence, there is one simple fact on which they cannot take a neutral position: The motivation of morality must be based on an absolute good. For morality to exist, there must be a standard of good. For there to be justice or injustice, right and wrong must be defined.

If there is no God, there is no absolute good, and your emotional pain is relative and irrelevant. However, the thing inside you that tells you something is wrong, the thing that has drawn you to read this book, is evidence of the Blueprint inside you. God has placed a clear scale of right and wrong inside you. Only an eternal God could have created such a wonderful Blueprint and clear measure of good that works so well.

BECOMING UNSTUCK

If the God factor is not resolved in your heart, the Blueprint falls apart. I have studied many arguments against this assertion, but none has created a replacement solution that works to free people from their torments and burdens. None! Show me the arguments. I'll show you God's Blueprint that works.

Find a Mentor

No matter what relationship you may have lacked in the first half of the Blueprint (the first four relationships), all is not lost. You have not lost your ability to have a relationship like that one, which will provide you with the tools you failed to acquire.

Alec was a very talented young man, good with his hands and hard-working. His wife and two little children adored him, and he tried hard at everything he did. You just couldn't paint a better family picture. But he came to me for mentoring because he wanted to grow; he wanted someone to be a father to him. He could see he needed to gain confidence, especially in how to be a good husband and business-man. He had moved his family down to Florida for various reasons, one being that he needed to leave the place where he grew up.

Gradually, I learned that he had been brought up by his mother, the "town whore" in their small community. He had extended family, including the grandfather who brought him up, whom he adored. This grandfather had given Alec his work ethic and manners, and taught him how to act as a man. Yet, when it came to raising his own family and being a husband, Alec seemed to have all sorts of leftover childish emotions. His grandfather had died, and he didn't have someone to advise him anymore.

One night as we were talking, I asked Alec about his father. "When I was growing up," he said, "My dad lived only two miles down the road with his new wife and kids but never came to see me."

Alec faced two huge blows: his parents' breakup and his father's seeming lack of care. The Blueprint says a father should be an active part of his son's life.

I then asked Alec to take me through a typical day in his childhood, and he described his routines of getting up, going to school, and returning home. Then he reached the part I immediately recognized as the moment when he had become emotionally frozen. "When I came home from school, I would run straight to my bedroom, close the door, jump into my closet, and play with my toys as quietly as I could."

"Why would you hide in the closet?"

"Because there were men who came over all the time to have sex with Mom, and I was scared of them."

Emotionally, Alec was still in that closet. How could we get him out?

"Sit on the couch, Alec, and answer when I call you," I told him.

I left the room, knocked on the door, and shouted, "Alec, are you in there?"

"Yes."

"I'm your dad, and I'm coming in." I walked over to the closet. "I'm opening up the door and taking you out of here." I opened the door, grabbed his hands, pulled him up, and hugged him, saying, "I'm sorry I wasn't here for you. I'm sorry I delayed coming and left you here. I should have come sooner."

Suddenly, Alec broke. This 250-pound grown man wept like a child. All the stored-up years of pain and anxiety came flooding out.

I told him to ask me "Where were you?" and as he did, the voice of a little boy spoke in both fear and frustration. Again, I apologized, but I assured him that I was opening the door and taking him out. The shoulder area of my shirt was soaking wet as this gentle giant let go of the past and let me lead him out of that emotional closet.

A mentor should have the relationship tools you need. If you don't have a father, find someone who has a father's heart. If you need a mother, find someone with a mother's heart. Likewise, if you need someone to be a big brother or sister, be bold and go find someone who can be that for you. It's not that they will be just the same as your father or mother or that they will do just what I have described, but they will relate to you in ways you still need.

This process may be difficult, because you have to also learn how to live as a son or daughter. When the Blueprint is followed, a son or daughter learns how to be loved, how to be corrected, how to be disciplined, how to be challenged, and how to be led—which will eventually enable them to grow up emotionally.

A good mentor will help you in all of these things. If you ask someone to fulfill that role for you and they can't, don't feel rejected. There are plenty of others out there. Your local church or synagogue should be able to help you find someone. Ask your friends whom they have as a life mentor, but don't be surprised if most don't have one at all.

Get What You Need

Chase down what you need. Many people learned as children that if they couldn't do something, they should just quit. Experience taught them to believe the ability or opportunity just wasn't there for them, or that they had no right to have what they wanted. They felt dejected, so they learned not to try at all. Even successful people will give up on something they feel is hopeless to pursue.

You must overcome this feeling of failure and push yourself to have your needs met. You must chase down the tools you need. You cannot allow the voice in your head to tell you it's not worth it—that's your childlike emotions talking. It *is* worth it, and you *must* get over your emotions and get the tools you need. It's a choice.

When you write, you probably write with only one of your hands. Most people sign their name with their right hand and do it effortlessly. Every day, we jot down notes, scribble out lists and sign our names without thinking about our ability to write. But if I asked you to start using your other hand, the one you don't use to write, you would find it a demanding task.

I would challenge you to try doing it right now. What you will experience is difficulty. It will feel uncomfortable. Your body will tense up. You may tire very quickly. Your brain will have to work harder to tell your hand what to do. Your writing will probably seem childlike, like you don't know how to write very well.

Trying to use new tools in your life will feel just like this. It will be difficult and discouraging at first, but you must keep working at it because eventually, it will pay off. You may not remember how you learned to write with your dominant hand when you were a child, but you did and became competent at writing. Learning to use new tools will be the same. The temptation will be to revert to using your default tools when you become tired and frustrated. But keep working at training yourself, and you will find that eventually, it will bring the better results that you really want.

There's an additional mentorship issue I must tackle with people: their response to being mentored. Typically, they either respond with rejection or respond with pride.

When I mentor someone, we often have to deal with the need to avoid feeling rejected if I, for example, don't answer their phone call, a common behavior. Not taking their call doesn't mean I don't want to talk to them, but that I can't or don't have the means to take that particular call. Then, when I don't hear from them in a timely manner, the person usually says they didn't call me because they didn't want to bug me and be a pain. I always tell them, "You need to accept the fact that I can decide for myself whether I can't or shouldn't take your call. I am mature enough to not allow myself to be controlled by you. I won't allow you to be a burden to me, so it's not possible for you to bug me in this regard."

This common respect and the ability to act as a mature adult safeguard a relationship and allow it to grow in a healthy manner. Don't back away from a good mentor. You must learn the way of pursuing a mentor as a child pursues his parent. Learn to pursue the tools you need.

As far as responding to mentorship with pride, most people don't see this in themselves. They truly think they have taken the advice they've been given, have it figured out, and don't need any more mentorship. But the problem is that these life-tools are not garnered in one conversation or one month of meet-ups. They are forged out of relationship and must be measured by the wise person giving them to you. Their years and experience will help you know how well you are doing.

Even professional athletes realize they must have constant coaching and measurement of their progress. They don't receive coaching only when they feel like it or when they can fit it into their schedule but make it a regular part of their life and routine. I know I have fallen prey to this problem, and I've learned you only recognize your pride once you arrive at the doorstep of pain. You go around the mountain once more, blindly using the wrong tools, only to repeat the same problem and end up with the same painful results.

Pride is a killer. You must pursue the tools you need. You must get yourself a coach, a mentor, a counselor. Don't allow pride to keep you from filling your backpack with the tools you still need.

The burden of getting what you need rests on your shoulders. It is not the responsibility of the mentor to treat you like a child and do everything for you. You cannot allow your own feelings of rejection or attitude of pride to stop you. Instead, you must train yourself to grow emotionally into an adult and get what you need from your mentor, trusting they can and will define the boundaries.

You will also find no one person has all the tools you need. One of the wonderful things about God is that He has given us different abilities. Each of us majors on something more than the next person. If you need mentoring in one particular skill or area, then find the person who has it to share.

You will remember I started this book with the story of how I shouted at God, "You're the worst-paying boss!" As my wife and I started having children, I realized I needed to get better at making money to not only sustain my family but build a future for them. I then started to feel the pain of my father having not taught me the intricacies of business. He taught me the great morals and character that undergird it, but business acumen just wasn't his thing. I went through a period of feeling dejected, not only because my father had already passed on but because I couldn't ask him what I should do to provide for my family. I ended up feeling frustrated and resentful.

One day, I attended a business seminar and asked the teacher if I could discuss some questions with him over lunch sometime. We met, and Rick became my business mentor from that day on. The crazy thing was that I had known and respected his success in business for ten years. But it took time for me to realize I was missing a tool in life, and I could now go to him to receive it. I didn't need to get the tool from my dad after all; I could find someone else.

My business mentor doesn't have to be a father to me in everything. I had a great dad. I was just missing the business tools. To this day, my mentor continues to give me more of those tools.

Notice that in this chapter, I have not told you what tools to find but rather, how to find them. Where do you find them? They are always hidden inside people. And God has a way of putting you in the path of the very people who have the tools you need.

You see, God has created this beautiful thing called the Blueprint. It's the way of family, of life. But it fundamentally needs relationship. In fact, the Blueprint is all about relationship: wonderful, functional, life-giving relationship. God, our loving Father, wants perfect relationship for us, because He designed us this way. That's why He created the Blueprint. Now, we need the tools to make it work.

CHAPTER 9

Last Word

Finding the tools you need

I vividly remember a moment with my father as he lay dying. I call it my orange juice moment because I recall this story every time I drink it.

Dad asked for some fresh orange juice, and I gladly fetched some for him. Wracked by the cancer, he couldn't sit up, so I held the glass with a straw so he could drink more easily. I was sitting in close to him, and he seemed to gulp the juice down as if he hadn't drunk in days. As he slurped the dregs, he let out a loud gasp and said, "Ahhh, that was good."

"That was good," he said.

This man whom we helplessly watched fade away, this man who had bitterly cried at the searing pain he endured, this man who would die in a few days still took a moment to say what was good.

But that's exactly the type of thing he had done my entire life. He had always taken moments throughout the day to say with his words what was good. He didn't wait for something amazing to happen before he used those words. He would live in the moment of what he had just experienced and speak something.

As I have matured, I have started to see how much my father used to speak words *prescriptively* first which then ended up as *descriptive* words thereafter. He chose to say that something was good even if he didn't feel it. If he was eating, driving, working, sweating, laughing, crying, persevering, coasting—whatever it was, he would always make a comment that it was good.

At the end of some of the days God created in the beginning, a phrase appears to describe God's reaction that I find significant for our lives: "It is good."

I believe in the power of words, and your words represent one of the biggest things that will change and should change in your journey to maturity. Words are either *descriptive* or *prescriptive*. *Descriptive* words convey or give an account of what is. *Prescriptive* words state what you want something to be.

Jesus spoke of both. He said your words come from the overflow of your heart. Whatever is in your heart will turn into words, and those words will manifest into your life, whatever good or bad they hold.

Your experiences build up memory and emotion inside you that make you feel good or bad. These emotions then turn into beliefs that fill up your heart. When you encounter a topic, issue, or event, you first feel your response in your heart through those pre-existing emotions. Your mind then converts those emotions into words that overflow from your mouth. We often think we speak logically, but we actually usually speak emotionally and call it logic. Those words are descriptive words. They firstly explain what you feel.

But in turn, those same words can become prescriptive words, because your words usually dictate your actions. How you choose to physically and relationally respond to the topic, issue, or event is directed by those emotions and beliefs spoken by your words. Proverbs

23:7a (KJV) says, "For as [a man] thinketh in his heart, so is he." You usually act out what you feel.

You have the choice to speak good or evil. At times, you descriptively speak what you feel inside that might be bad. But those same words can turn into a prescription for how you continue to believe and act.

If you say it, you will most likely end up truly believing it. For example, if you say it is useless to find a mentor, because that's how you feel, your actions will follow in that belief. You won't work hard to find a mentor. This is why it is so important to have your heart changed. Let it grow up into maturity and start speaking what is good, right, and true instead of how you feel.

Today, people who can't stop their feelings from overcoming what they truly want in life will submit themselves to someone else who uses words to tell them what to do. Just go to your local gymnasium. There are thousands of people who are paying personal trainers thousands of dollars to simply tell them to do what they already know they should and can do. But because their hearts are full of negative emotions about exercise, they know they will talk themselves out of doing that workout. So, they pay money and give that power of descriptive, positive commands to someone else.

Speaking good was a powerful tool my dad put in my backpack, and I only realized its worth years after his death. I believe God has left tools for us through our families and other great people in our lives that we may have not seen because we were still stuck at some other emotional impasse. As you move on emotionally, you will learn to see some of the tools you need were, in fact, given to you, but you didn't realize you had them. I discovered my dad's prescriptive words years after he died, and they are now tools in my hands.

All the finest, wisest, and most mature men and women I know are people who understand they must continue to be learning, obedient, spiritual sons and daughters in the faith themselves. They know how to humble themselves as a child and yet lead as a seasoned father or mother.

One of my greatest mentors and examples of this is my father-in-law, who not only passes on great tools to me but makes efforts to obtain them himself. One of his finest character qualities is that he purposefully pursues being mentored even when it would be easier to rest on his well-deserved laurels. I take note of his response when he has to work to learn as a son from the spiritual father in his life. When he has disagreed, failed to understand, or endured the pain of doing what his mentor has asked, he has responded as an obedient son. You won't get to see it in him unless you are acting as a son or daughter to him, however, because only sons and daughters see these deeper things in their parents.

The common denominator I have found in every mentor I have ever had is this: None of them were trying to become great people. Instead, they were trying to become the best son or daughter they could be, for this is the only role where we are entirely fulfilled. It's the completion of the Blueprint: to walk with God the Father. The family God has placed you in is only a practice run for the greater relationship to which we must all return—the one our father and mother, Adam and Eve, had. God has designed us to walk with Him as a son or daughter walks with their father.

Who is your father or mother today? Maybe it's your real mum or dad; maybe it's someone who is not. Regardless, you still need that parental figure, and you still need to chase them to get the rest of your tools for life.

They will help you to walk with God once again. They will help you to build your life and family according to the Blueprint God has designed families to follow. His Blueprint is for your success. His Blueprint can un-screw up your family. His Blueprint works.

Are you ready to try it?

End Notes

Introduction—The Day I Found a Gap

1. "blueprint," Collins English Dictionary, British English definition, accessed December 1, 2018, https://www.collinsdictionary.com/us/dictionary/english/blueprint.

Chapter 1—The Blueprint Revealed

1. "Marriage and Divorce, U.S.," Fast Stats Homepage, Centers for Disease Control and Prevention, accessed December 1, 2018, https://www.cdc.gov/nchs/fastats/marriage-divorce.htm.; "Number, Timing, and Duration of Marriages and Divorces: 2009—Detailed Tables," United States Census Bureau, accessed December 1, 2018, https://www.census.gov/data/tables/2009/demo/marriage-and-divorce/p70-125.html.

2. Studies conflict as to whether or not we are happier or not. It seems so relative. But I firmly believe most people, especially those who are now in their latter years, are not saying relationships are happier today. If anything, they are saying the opposite.

3. "Measuring National Well-Being: Life in the U.K., 2012," Office for National Statistics, accessed December 1, 2018, https://

webarchive.nationalarchives.gov.uk/20160106192925/http://
www.ons.gov.uk/ons/dcp171766_287415.pdf. Figure 2 notes
that life satisfaction changed little both during years of rising
GDP and the recession of 2008; "How Are Canadians Really Doing?" Canadian Index of Wellbeing, 2012 CIW Report,
https://uwaterloo.ca/canadian-index-wellbeing/sites/ca.cana-
dian-index-wellbeing/files/uploads/files/HowareCanadiansre-
allydoing_CIWnationalreport2012.pdf, accessed Feb. 23, 2019.
Over a seventeen-year period from 1994 to 2010, Canada's GDP
grew by 28.9 percent while quality of life only improved by 5.7
percent; "Wealth and Happiness Revisited," Michael R. Hag-
erty and Ruut Veenhoven, *Social Indicators Research*, https://
personal.eur.nl/veenhoven/Pub2000s/2003e-full.pdf, accessed
Feb. 22, 2019. Authors note that increased happiness is tied
with the needs theory, which implies that citizens had unmet
needs that could be gratified by goods and services, though
with diminishing marginal utility of income. That is to say,
once a person reaches a certain income that meets their needs,
their happiness didn't increase thereafter with income increase.

4. Rev. Timothy Keller, "The Still Small Voice," sermon delivered at
Redeemer Presbyterian Church, September 26, 1999; Gospel in
Life podcast accessed December 1, 2018, https://gospelinlife.
com/downloads/the-still-small-voice-8969/.

Chapter 3—The First Four Relationships

1. Louis Matthews Sweet, *The Birth and Infancy of Jesus Christ*
(Philadelphia: Westminster, 1906), 188; "Parthogenesis," Wiki-
pedia, https://en.wikipedia.org/wiki/Parthenogenesis, accessed
February 23, 2019.

2. Chris Bell, *"Huhu Animation win lucrative six-part US Series,"* The Big Idea Charitable Trust, January 19, 2007, https://www.thebigidea.nz/node/174771, accessed Feb. 23, 2019.

3. James Strong, S.T.D., LL.D., *Strong's Exhaustive Concordance of the Bible* (Madison, New Jersey: World Bible Publishers, 1989), *Hebrew & Chaldee Dictionary of the OT 1847* from root 3045: to ascertain by *seeing*.

4. Covenant with creation: Genesis 8:22; Genesis 9:1-17. Covenant with a man: Genesis 12:1-3, 14. 15. 17. Covenant with a people: Exodus 19:3-6, 20. Covenant with royalty: 2 Samuel 7:12-13. Covenant with Christ: Jeremiah 31:31-34. 5. "covenant," http://www.merriam-webster.com/dictionary/covenant, accessed Feb. 23, 2019.

6. Strong, *Strong's Exhaustive Concordance, Hebrew & Chaldee Dictionary of the OT 1285* from 1262 to *select* (in the sense of *cutting* [like 1254 to *create*]); a *compact* (because made by passing between *pieces* of flesh): confederacy, covenant, league. 7. Nicholas A. Smith and Laurel J. Trainor "Infant-Directed Speech Is Modulated by Infant Feedback," *Infancy* (2008) 13:4, 410-420, DOI: 10.1080/15250000802188719.

8. "Father Factor," National Fatherhood Initiative, https://www.fatherhood.org/father-absence-statistic, accessed February 23, 2019; "Dad Stats," National Responsible Fatherhood Clearinghouse, https://www.fatherhood.gov/content/dad-stats, accessed February 23, 2019.

9. John Eldredge, *Fathered by God* (Nashville, Tennessee: Thomas Nelson, 2009).

Chapter 4—The Last Three Relationships

1. "Marriage and Child Wellbeing Revisited," *The Future of Children*, Princeton-Brookings, Vol. 25, No. 2 (Fall 2015), https://futureofchildren.princeton.edu/sites/futureofchildren/files/media/marriage_and_child_wellbeing_revisited_25_2_full_journal.pdf, accessed February 23, 2019; Glenn T. Stanton, "Family Formation and Poverty: A History of Academic Inquiry and Its Major Findings," *The Family in America* (Fall 2015), http://familyinamerica.org/files/3214/5806/3564/Stanton.pdf, accessed February 23, 2018; *Why Marriage Matters, Third Edition: Thirty Conclusions from the Social Sciences* (Institute for American Values, 2011).

2. Strong, *Strong's Exhaustive Concordance*, Publishers, 1989), *Hebrew & Chaldee Dictionary of the OT* 120: *ruddy*, i.e. a *human being* (an individual or the species, *mankind*, etc.); Ronald Hendel, "Adam" Entry in David Noel Freedman, *Eerdmans Dictionary of the Bible* (Grand Rapids, Michigan: Wm. B. Eerdmans Publishing Co., 2000), 18-19.

3. "Father Absence + Involvement Statistics," National Fatherhood Initiative, http://www.fatherhood.org/media/fatherhood-statistics, accessed February 23, 2019; *Charting Parenthood: A Statistical Portrait of Fathers and Mothers in America*, Child Trends, 2002, https://www.childtrends.org/wp-content/uploads/2013/03/ParenthoodRpt2002.pdf, accessed February 23, 2019. "Married adults are much more likely than single adults to be living with their own minor children, though the percentages differ substantially by gender. Among those who are not married, 11 percent of men and 29 percent of females live with their own child. Among those who are married, 54 percent of

men and 56 percent of women live with at least one of their own children."

4. Laura Schlessinger, *Ten Stupid Things Men Do to Mess Up Their Lives* (New York, HarperCollins, 1997). 5. Dr. Phil McGraw, "Identify Bad Guys with Dr. Phil's 8 Warning Signs," Oprah's Lifeclass, Oprah Winfrey network, video, https://www.youtube.com/watch?v=WIx4nZWvxkE, accessed February 23, 2019.

Chapter 5—The First Half Affects the Second Half

1. Kathryn Edin and Timothy J. Nelson, *Doing the Best I Can: Fatherhood in the Inner City* (Berkeley and Los Angeles, California: University of California Press, 2013).

2. "New Research on Inner City Fathers, "The Diane Rehm Show," http://thedianerehmshow.org/shows/2013-05-28/new-research-inner-city-fathers/transcript, accessed March 15, 2019.

Chapter 6—Three-Step Roadmap: Step One, Deal with the Root

1. *National Geographic: Stress—Portrait of a Killer* (Los Angeles: 20th Century Fox, 2008).

2. Paul Tough, *How Children Succeed* (New York: Houghton Mifflin Harcourt Publishing Company, 2012).

3. Strong, *Strong's Exhaustive Concordance, Greek Dictionary of the NT* 863 from root 575.

Made in the USA
Lexington, KY
06 December 2019